Embers

Embers

a novel in poems

TERRY WOLVERTON

Susan,
Thank you so much
for your extraordinary
support of my
work.
In gratitude,
Terry

RED HEN PRESS LOS ANGELES

EMBERS
Copyright © 2003 Terry Wolverton

Cover Design: Susan Silton, SoS Los Angeles

Book Design: Mark E. Cull

ISBN 1-888996-72-2
Library of Congress Catalog Card Number: 2003093916
Manufactured in Canada

Publication of this volume is made possible in part
through support by the California Arts Council.

Red Hen Press
www.redhen.org

First Edition

This is a work of fiction about people who actually lived. Some still do. Where the author knew them, she has used real names. Many of the events described took place, although perhaps not as they have been rendered here. It is certain that others perceived them differently. Some events were invented by the author when factual information could not be obtained. The texture of events, as well as the characters' psychologies and motivations are entirely the work of the author's imagination and thus are intended to represent *her* truth, not necessarily the truth of those who lived these experiences.

They walk inside me. This blood
is a map of the road between us.
I am why they survived.
The world behind them did not close.
The world before them is still open.
All around me are my ancestors . . .

From "Tear,"
Linda Hogan, *The Book of Medicines*

. . . our Ancestors need to be healed . . .

Ancestors: Hidden Hands, Healing Spirits
For Your Use and Empowerment
written through Min. Ra Ifagbemi Babalawo

Many of the Huron . . . sought refuge among the Tionontati . . . Soon, however [they] were driven out of Southern Ontario by the Iroquois . . . . . . the survivors, about eight hundred in number, came to be known as the Wyandot, a corruption of Wendat, the former name of the Huron confederacy. . . . In 1701, the French persuaded the Wyandot to settle close to Fort Ponchartrain, which was being built near Detroit . . .

— Bruce G. Trigger, *The Huron: Farmers of the North*

CONTENTS

BOOK TWO : 1957 – 2000

Timeline

1907	Marie Girard born.
1910	Maries father dies.
1918	Marie's mother remarries.
1919	Marie leaves home.
1921	Marie impregnated by Fraiser.
1921	Arthur born, son of Marie and Fraiser.
1921	Marie marries Michael McCarthy.
1922	Richard is born, son of Marie & McCarthy.
1924	Marie leaves McCarthy for Adolph Young, takes Arthur with her, leaves Richard behind.
1925	Marie divorces McCarthy, marries Adolph Young. Catholic Church refuses to grant annulment; Marie is excommunicated.
1926	Frank is born, son of Marie & Young.
1932	*Ruth Miller is born, daughter of Elsba and Charles Miller.*
1933–35	Arthur and Frank put into foster care when Marie and Adolph are unable to feed them.
1937	Marie sets her house on fire.
1937	Marie is incarcerated in Eloise Hospital for the Insane (she will be in and out of this hospital for the next 40 years.)
1939	Arthur marries Irene; marriage is annulled later this same year.
1941	Arthur enlists in the Army Air Corps.
1942	Arthur marries Verda.
1943	Arthur captured in Germany, incarcerated as a prisoner of war.
1946	Judy is born, daughter of Arthur and Verda.
1948	Jeff is born, son of Arthur and Verda.
1952	*Ruth marries Don Wolverton.*
1954	Arthur and Verda divorced.
1954	*Terry is born, daughter of Ruth and Don.*
1955	*Ruth and Don divorced.*
1956	Arthur marries Mary.
1957	Patrick is born, son of Arthur and Mary.
1958	Arthur and Mary divorce.
1959	Arthur marries Ruth.

1962	Arthur and Richard meet in jail.
1974	*Terry drops out of college.*
1976	*Terry moves to California.*
1977	Marie dies.
1978	*Elsba dies.*
1978	Arthur and Ruth divorce.
1981	Eloise Hospital for the Insane closes its doors.
1981	Adolph dies.
1985	Frank dies.
1995	Arthur dies.
1995	Jeff dies.

PROLOGUE

LEGACY

1.

Marie's soul paces Afterlife
like a long hallway,
soles barely sounding on scarred
linoleum. She
scuffs past pea green walls, digs at
whisper-dry wicks
of hangnails, puffs phantom
cigarettes. Smoke swirls
to elusive heaven. Feet
shuffle toward EXIT

sign, dim red glow receding
with each step. What haunts
her is what's left unreconciled:
wet wounds trespassed,
offspring left behind, priest's black
slammed gate, bland doctor's
searing verdict. Who among
the living might take up
her cause, unlatch the bolt on
limbo's heavy door?

2.

Earth does not forget.
It drinks the soot of cook fires,
swill of afterbirth.
Records hard stamp of moccasins.
Collects the singsong
chants and taunts of children's games,
lovers' rough whispers.
Bones sink into dirt's embrace,
their restless secrets
ever coded in that place.

Life is a river,
its ceaseless flux. Forest yields
to fortress, then a
city rises in its stead.
New arrivals swell
the factories, stoke internal
combustion.
Language vanishes, and with
it, stories die like
cinders. Still, land remembers.

3.

Is blood the only
thread with which to stitch our past
to future, ensure
the body's code is carried
forward, vast river
in which history, with all
its obligations,
can roil and hitch itself to
innocence? Are genes
the only vessels fit to

bestow the blueprint?
Or might ether, nurture, dreams
be other means
of linkage? Perhaps it's passed through
air, like smoke, or touch –
rough hand on child's forehead
yokes two souls – a shared
mad gleam in a winking eye?
And once the bond is
formed, an ancestor is born.

The Origin of the Snake Clan

Grandmother built the hut
herself. Such a frail
woman, spine a crooked
stem; still she stripped
bark from cedar, stretched
it over wood, gathered
round stones for a fire pit
in her shuddering hands.

She instructed me to wait
here alone until power
found me. It was winter,
my breath was blue. She left
no food. My raw belly
was a cavern of dreams;
I swam in its black pools
as moons climbed the sky.

Time swallowed its own tail.
When Snake appeared, my fire
went out, leaving only a coil
of smoke. He swayed beside
me, tongued my hunger. Taunted,
"If your people do not feed you soon
I will claim you as my own."
When Grandmother returned,
her pockets were empty of meat.

She was too old to run
home on twig legs across ice,
too late to fetch a hunk of fish,
a handful of corn from the larder.
I was already changing: my two
legs fused into a thick ribbon
of muscle, skin beginning
to gleam; tears unthawed
the frozen ground, a deepening pool.

Sun chased darkness as my people
gathered on the shore
of their new lake; grandmother's
hut submerged in its depths.
She huddled with her tribe,
and seemed to shrivel as I rose
from the water's belly, entwined
with Snake, my partner, my fate.

BOOK ONE

1919–1959

1919 ~ Marie
ORPHAN

One's family can disappear
inside a whispered curse,
one's house dissolve into a gray street,
leave its daughter
orphaned, only the memory
of a stepfather's hands

slithering over fevered skin, hands
like snakes that seem to disappear
beneath her garments, memory
of lace, hiss of curses
murmured like prayer into a daughter's
neck, sour stench of the street

uncoiling on his tongue, those streets
from which her true father sheltered her, his hands
that built this house for wife and daughter
before his life disappeared,
breath drained in one suspended curse,
leaving empty walls and prayers and memory.

But here, her memory
blurs: mother come in from dismal street
to find a serpent in her bed, the curse
bled from her tongue cut deeper than hands
that strafe a young girl's face until all disappear –
house, lace, mother, daughter.

Then she's no one's daughter;
house sinks in memory,
rooms dissolve and disappear
into this city where she plods the streets,
twelve years old, hands
numb to chill curse

of Midwest February. She learns to curse
men who seek in her some lost daughter,
molding her beneath their hands
as if to conjure memory.
Hunger keeps her stalking gray streets,
snow falls like lace, a place to disappear.

Prayers or curses, spark of memory
dims inside a daughter of the streets –
rub your hands together, child, so your flame won't disappear.

1919 ~ Detroit

CITY OF SALT

A ghostly city with its own network of
four-lane highways lies deep beneath the
industrial heart of Detroit, its crystalline
walls glittering and gleaming in the flickering
light. It is a world of no night or day. It is
a world of salt.
                  – Patricia Zacharias, *The Detroit News*

Once this was the sea. Woodward Avenue
was brine; Gratiot nothing but the pull
of tide. No trolleys or factories, no
maple trees. Four million years ago
an ocean died, blood evaporated.
Salt is its bones, interred by glacier.
Marie saunters over those bones; they crunch
beneath her worn heels as she stares into
rock-hard eyes of passing men. Some look back;
she stands unmoving as a pillar. Twelve
hundred feet below, ropes lower mules down
the shaft; they stay in the salt mines until
they die. Marie turns up her collar. Fine
snow sprinkles the sidewalk, reeks of the sea.

The Customer

He didn't want a virgin,
he insisted to the bartender,
all that mess, that blood.

He didn't want some child
to cringe before him
like a struck mutt.

He didn't want an orphan
whose scrawny limbs
looked lean enough to snap.

What kind of man
d'you take me for?
He wanted a woman, a woman's twat,

round and warm to take him in,
not a raw girl to break
into, like a common thief.

What d'you mean, she's all y've got?
He thumped his fist against the bar.
I'd sooner have my wife!

The bartender was pragmatic,
a businessman. He winked,
One hole's just like another,

and slid a bottle neck between
his lips. The customer saw reason:
he required relief. Why bother

to undress? *All right,* he shrugged,
I'll take the girl, and pushed
two shiny coins across the bar.

The barkeep tucked one
in his apron pocket,
flipped the other for

the girl to catch. He gestured
toward the back room.
The customer led her there

and made her kneel. He did not trouble
to caress her dirty face, or whisper
any kindness in her ear.

Don't bite, he cautioned
with a warning fist,
and then unzipped,
and took his satisfaction.

1919 ~ Marie

First Blow Job

Was it lust or resignation?
A young girl's curiosity
or hunger's calculation
that made the twelve-year-old Marie
take the man's distended member
in her unwashed mouth?

The architecture of his face,
the rough wood floor that scraped her knees
while tinny, barroom tunes erased
the music of his moan and wheeze –
none of this would she remember
in the aftermath.

As she clutched her crucifix or
gripped his silver dollar in her fist,
as she drank the thick elixir
that burned inside her throat, like piss,
did God see all she surrendered
as she choked for breath?

THE MENTOR

Honey, I seen 'em younger
than you, but most of 'em
had a little more meat
on their bones. Got to give
a man somethin' to grab
onto – a handful
to squeeze. That's what they like.
Got to get the hungry
off you – reminds 'em too much
of their own troubles.
What you're sellin's a few minutes
of sweet forgetfulness – you mind
that now. Sometimes a man
likes company at dinner, good
way to get a free plate
of grub. Though, green
as you are, how you gonna
entertain him with your talk?

You got a heap to learn,
girl, cain't study it
on the job. I could teach
you tricks – where to use
your teeth, the magic words
to sigh into their bellies –
make 'em keep comin'
back to you. Steady customers,
that's what you want
in this business, less chance
of gettin' slapped around
or cut. I got men what bring
me presents on my birthday,
regular as the sun. What – love?
Honey, what you do on that mattress
ain't nothin' to do with love,
no matter what they scream
out in the dark.

Now I shown you how to take
a rag all up inside you,
swab yourself clean. Vinegar's
best, but a little Coca Cola'll
work too, even some cold
coffee if it's black. Whiskey
burns if you don't water it down.
Got to dig up what they plant,
girl, don't give it no chance
to take root. The minute
your garden grows, you're outta
business. Naw, the Church
don't like it, but they ain't fond
of anything 'bout the likes of us.
Starvin' won't get you
to heaven, remember that.
Just listen to old Calcutta, hear,
and do like I say.

FRAISER

To her, he would always smell of summertime

     not the heavy stink of the working men

     who trudged in, shift-weary, August caked into grime

     at their collars, butcher's blood or axle grease wedged

     under fingernails, no one to wash for

     not so long ago she'd lain beneath them, or ones

     just like them, taste of August and scarce wages on their sour

     tongues; now she stood behind the polished bar, poured beer

     with a thick head, let their jokes slide off her like foam

new cut grass, fields of chicory, Queen Anne's lace

     scorched nights he'd hunch in a back booth, cupping

     a leatherbound book; how she envied the pages that held

     his blue gaze, how she captured it just a moment as she served

     his whiskey; the only man she knew who read

     the only man to enter her who said, "I love you"

     in his Scotsman's lilt; what he planted in her

     she vowed to bring to season, but come autumn,

     he was gone, she left to harvest alone

his red-gold beard like sunrise above her

his eyes like an open sky

ANOTHER BARTENDER'S STORY

Over time you grow used to the smell,
sharp as cologne but not sweet,
more like something half-digested,
sour rot that seeps into skin.
Each night you carry it
back through the gas-lit streets
to your small room, already gray
and gloomy with the threat

of morning. Home from the Great War,
you turned your back on Ford's assembly
lines, sunk your savings into this small
place, gave your name to it like a son,
relieved to spend your days
in cool, continual twilight,
in the company of other broken men,
while the nickelodeon leaked

music. You should have shoo'd her away
the first time she poked her scrawny
shoulders through the double doors.
When she told her age, you knew
she was lying, still you nodded,
put her to work, taught her to rasp
ice, to scrub the cuspidors, shake salt
into washwater to make the glassware

shine. She wasn't as strong as
the Colored men you hired
to haul boxes of bright bottles,
still, she earned her keep, grateful
for the dinner meal of meat and gravy,
the pallet in the storage room.
But she was just a kid, too trusting
of the easy kindness from a handsome

mouth. By the time she confessed
to you, she was already swollen
with Fraiser's child, and the scoundrel
long gone. It wasn't your dream, a quick
trip before dour priest, no white dress
and no organ, only hushed vows
of necessity. Some days you'd read
her eyes in the dim barlight, still

hungering. He should have been a bastard
but you gave your family name to the boy
who screamed out of her, red-skinned
and sticky, and later a second son,
she swore this one was yours. He's
the one she left when she disappeared,
her wedding ring in the top drawer,
your son in the crib, the smell of alcohol

seeped into memory. The nickelodeon
trills a lullaby. Now your dreams
are glass, tumblers and goblets,
punch cups and schooners, glinting
in continual twilight, and each
must be filled. Ambers and oranges,
absinthe and burgundy. You spend your hours
pouring color, watch it drain away.

THE MAN IN THE FELT HAT

He belonged to the world
of daylight. A man in
a felt hat. Quick smile
on the street car. The neat
mustache. Clean fingernails.
Not strapping like her husband.
Not tall. More like her.
The best thing about Adolph
was: she didn't meet him
in the bar.
                    That night he
took her dancing. Hand light
on her waist. She inhaled
the starch of his pressed shirt.
Perfume of shoe polish,
aftershave. Reading like Braille
the nap of good wool.
Her own skin stunk of beer
scum, sour milk and ash.
She left him quick. Scurried
back to the bar
                    alone
in the endless dusk. She
hummed all day. Some bright tune
the band had played. Squinting
beyond the double doors.
To catch a crack of sunlight.
Some afternoons she walked
to Woodward Avenue.
The store where Adolph
worked.

Peered into plate glass.
Past her own reflection.
His father, stern beside
the register. Displays
of pumps and t-straps, suede
and silk. Poised on stands
like jewels. Fingered by
stylish customers. Furs
loosened at their throats. Genteel,
with coy smiles and greedy
eyes.
　　The window mirrored
her: hair blowzy, nose red
in the chill air. Her own shape
swallowed in her husband's
shapeless coat. But young still,
just sixteen. When he looked
up at her and grinned,
she beamed back. Unashamed.
His customer unshod,
he rose to greet her. While
his father glowered.
　　　　　　　　Her
husband shattered bottles
till the bar glittered. Wrecked
their bedroom. Flung dresses
to the sidewalk. Where they
bloomed. An early garden.
His furious bouquet. Her
oldest boy helped gather
them. Her youngest howled
in an upstairs room. As
she fled her twilit life.

DISINHERITANCE

At first he was relieved
to be out of the business
of shoes, released
from an assembly line
of feet – bunioned or callused,
ticklish, odoriferous,
hiding a darn in the stocking
and always seeking
more compact housing,
toes cramped, heels pinched
in plaintive vanity:
"Let me have these
in a smaller size."

Something unmanly then,
to be always kneeling
at a woman's hem, he'd muse
as he drove each dawn
to the construction site
to break his tender hands
on brick, learn grace
on scaffolding and how to drive
a nail true. His skin
reddened in the days'
relentless light, crusted with grit
and sawdust, a shell
armoring the gentle man.

Only after weeks of gashes
on his skin and forearms,
swollen fingers, muscles
that cramped and spasmed
in his sleep, sputum
thickened with dust
that settled everywhere,
in his hair, between his teeth,
unrelieved by a cold beer at noon,
as the pain in his hands
went unrelieved by nightly

soaking, and exhaustion weighed
beneath the surface of the skin

only then did he question
his promise: he'd do anything
to have her, defy his proud
father and weeping mother,
turn his back on shoes, only
then did life stretch before
him like the ladders
he'd learned to climb, legs
heavier with each ascending
step, rungs shuddering
beneath his fragile girth
and seeming to extend forever
into hot blue glare.

1925 ~ Marie
COMMON LAW

Adolph had no use for priests
so she went alone to the
cathedral to petition
the monsignor. Fingering

one fraying strap of her thin
pocketbook, she stood before
the straight-spined priest and fixed her
gaze on the gray veins that branched

the marble floor. Stale incense
hung in the air like a ghost,
clotted her throat; his voice droned
the sanctity of wedlock:

Law was paper, easily
torn, but the Church was bedrock.
Her divorce shred like onion-
skin against his granite tongue.

The black-frocked father perched, a
somber raven at pew's edge.
Beyond him, in the distance,
Christ dangled from the cross, eyes

blank, expression bored. He too
had noticed her threadbare coat,
shoe heels worn round; annulment
wasn't for the likes of her,

whose grubby hands would never
feed the coffers. He almost
smiled as if approving when
the priest's clipped "Impossible!"

scissored the cord of ever-
lasting life, her pleas falling,
scraps of tissue in the thick
air. Her eyes were stung by ash,

flames erupted at her feet,
reddening her cheeks, licking
the hem of her best dress. It
was then she knew she would burn.

Failed Conversion

Father Jean is a curiosity.
White hairs plummet from his chin
like a rain shower
and his eyes are pale
as a stream at winter's thaw.
His thick tongue stumbles
on broken legs
through my people's language,
hops nimble as a child
over the low music of his own.

His powers are mysterious
and great: he captures
stories in flat bundles
he calls "books," traps
the arc of light and darkness
on a wheel. When its spirit
cries out, the old priest
consults the wheel
and nods, but never
sets time free.

I go to his cabin
at the edge of the forest;
my eyes swell
with strangeness: his vessel
for food; the heavy robes
that weight bone and conceal
flesh; thin sticks that mark
pressed sheets of birch,
leave their trails
of black blood.

I want to learn to make
those scratches, to scan
their meaning; that's why
I come. He tells me stories
of his Jesus, says I must
bow down to the god

who bound his only
child to a crossed tree,
left him to bleed. I tell
him this is not our way.

He warns that I must give
up dreaming – might as well
relinquish water or breath.
What use is a spirit
who speaks through books
that only some can read,
instead of visiting the sleep
of each, each night
revealing to us more
of our desires?

Father Jean goes too far,
wants to lash his cross
to the pallet where I lie
with my husband, to blanket
us with Laws. He demands
we trap time in a gold circle,
fingers bound forever.
What god commands us
to surrender freedom, cage
love inside an everlasting vow?

1926 – Adolph

FRANK'S BIRTH

When that baby
squalled, red and blue
and sticky, squeezed
from the slit hole
of her, you thought
you'd be proud,
at last an heir
to the family
name, no longer
patched to some other
man's bastard.

But from the start,
something was wrong –
scrawny arms, legs,
a mewling, puny
boy; it made you
sick to watch him
gnaw his mother's
breast, touch the thin
membrane stretched across
his skull, catch his
flailing fist.

Two robust sons
she gave to other
men. To you, this
milk-eyed boy with skin
like parchment, startled
by loud voices,
scared of roughhouse
play, no better
than a damn girl.
A whining insult.
A permanent rebuke.

LOST BOY

1. Richard

Although his poppa told him to forget,
he never stopped waiting for his mother
to come home. He grew pale in the bar's gloom,
fattened on bowls of pickles and sardines,
salted nuts; his friends, the shambling men who
propped themselves on stools or slumped in back booths,
dozing. To each he showed the photograph:
a young woman, staring past the lens; they'd
shrug and mutter in their beer. Not even
the cops, who came 'round each week to collect,
could tell him where to find his lost mother.
Pop scoffed, "She left when you were small, you don't
remember," but the boy insisted he
recalled a blue dress, and the smell of smoke.

2. Marie

Who is the patron saint of lost children,
those round-eyed buggers gaping into air,
mouths gone slack and noses plugged with snot? Who
sees after their teeth and broken bones, darns
the stocking holes and scrubs behind their ears?
These cast-off brats who're spent like coins, bartered
for a mother's freedom. Always bawling
when I try to sleep, fists tugging the hem
of my nightgown. Haunting my dreams, forlorn
ghost with questions dripping from his eyes. I
hope some angel's watching out for him. *Bless
me, Father, for I've sinned* . . . My husband had
a bruising temper; if I'd tried to take
his son, he never would'a let me go.

1931 ~ Arthur

PET

The parakeet's eye
is a cold black seed
behind wires that slice
its view. A finger
slipped between the bars,
a beak closed over
the tip, never fierce
enough to draw blood.

      The boy's bum stung, soft hole burning
      a smoldering rose. Empty now
      he felt still full, small opening
      stretched, stuffed, split like petals.

The parakeet preens
in watery beam
of winter sunlight
spilled through cloudy panes.
Airless feathers. Blue
wings remain unfanned.
Its warble swallowed
in the room's thick hush.

      His father was gone now, the man
      he called father, gone in a blast
      of cold air, screen door slam. The boy
      regathered his trousers.

Unlatches the cage.
Finger offered, claws
accept the perch. Boy
sinks to the floor, curls
beneath cage. Down belly
pressed warm to his cheek,
a faint light washes
him, bars stripe his skin.

1932 ~ Marie

Anniversary

She'd been hoping for carnations or perfume
sheathed in bright wrapping, bound with a satin bow,
a mirror to show her what she meant to him.

Their nights – once full of romance and spoon;
he'd gaze at her as if she were aglow
and lavish her with violets and perfume.

Now too many evenings found her lonesome,
coaxing crackly music from the radio;
she'd wait and wonder what she meant to him.

The weight of worry threatened to consume
their love: always too many bills, not enough dough,
none left to spare for daisies or perfume.

She supposed no marriage could remain a honeymoon
nor keep alive that spark from long ago,
the radiance of what she'd meant to him.

Still, when he gave his gift to her: bucket and broom,
chagrin erupted, compelled her throw
it at his head and chase him from their room
where she keened bitterness like a lost canto

Not just the dearth of roses and perfume
but the drudgery of what she meant to him.

—◠◠—

Invisible Journey

. . . every Huron was believed to have a soul that was possessed of concealed but very powerful desires. Sometimes these desires were revealed . . . in . . . dreams. . . . If those desires remained unfulfilled, the soul became angry and would cause its owner to suffer illness and misfortune.

— Bruce G. Trigger, *The Huron: Farmers of the North*

Each night I leave behind
the toil of daylight —
grit of ground corn
under my fingernails,
scent of salt fish on my palms.
My back no longer bent
with digging, stooped
to plant or gather wood
for the hearth fire.

At night I close my eyes,
lay my flesh down
so that my soul can walk
the long road unburdened.
Soft sand slips beneath
cracked heels, cools, scent
of new grass guides me
to the river, where the moon
leans over my shoulder.

Each night the old woman
meets me; her braids gleam
silver in the moon's glow
and from around her neck,
shells drip like stars.
She squats on the bank, opens
her arms, rocks me
like an infant, croons
the words to an old song.

I can never remember
the long walk home, crickets
fading as sun drives moon
from the sky. I awaken
to the crackle of new flame
on the hearth, my pallet
beside my husband. He rises
without greeting or embrace.
My lungs ache with fever.

1932 ~ Detroit

BREAD

All morning she waits in line
that never seems to move or
shorten; stained pavement beneath
her thin soles leaches an ache
into her calves and hips. Her
worn, shapeless coat, hair unstyled –
street filled with women like her

and children with the same tight
eyes, pinched faces. Her own boys
at home: Frank, the youngest, howls
beside the cold stove. Just five,
he can't explain the gnawing
in his belly, the milk cup
empty, his whimpers ignored.

Not like Art, her oldest, who
rummages for scraps in trash
bins, brings her treats: half-eaten
apple, brown flesh pared away;
partly smoked cigarette, red
lip prints on the filter. Who
tries to coax carrots, lettuce

out of backyard dirt, shoulders
wincing above the spade. He
glowers at Adolph, slumped at
table, another day spent
outside the Ford plant, chain of
men, big hands hung slack, idleness
eating them like ulcer;

foreman makes them stand in line
for hours, then sends them home: "No
jobs." At night Adolph mutters
into her pillow, "We can't
feed them, Marie, we've got to
let the foster people take
them." Repeats it till she cries.

Some women let their children
wait in line; she never does.
Rises in half-light, slips on
her thin coat, takes her place on
crowded sidewalk. Still, some days
she's too late; trudges home with
empty hands, empty pockets.

Today, though, she grabs her prize,
hefts the loaf in hand, cradles
it like an infant, yeast scent
rising from coat. Mouth waters,
but she resists urge to tear
hunks of crust, feed her own sour
gullet. Means to keep her boys.

Foster Care

Each house smells of strangers:
cabbage boiling on the stove,
harsh soap at the rim of the sink,
starched sheets that scrape
against the skin in bed,
hard pillows shaped
by someone else's head,
rotting bananas, sweaty feet and dust.

Each time we come to a new place
I try to hide one shirt
beneath the mattress
just to keep the smell of home.
Sometimes they find it,
squeeze it through the wringer;
hid long enough, the cloth absorbs
the air around it, loses its memories.

My brother smells like sour milk,
unwashed armpits and the school paste
he eats. He cries
when they hit us; I never do.
Each night I hear
his sniffles soak the pillow.
Come morning, I grab the damp case,
hold it to my nose and breathe.

FACTORY SONG

Skinny boy in a man's work boots,
at sixteen you leave school, scent
of chalk and varnish, scarred wooden desks,
lined paper slick beneath your palms.

At sixteen you leave school, sent
out into the world to earn a paycheck;
you trade lined paper, cool beneath your palms
for a lunch box, a time card, a wage.

Your folks need the extra paycheck
so you rise at four a.m. to ride the streetcar.
A lunch box, a time card, a wage –
you hire on at the tire factory.

Four a.m. view through streetcar windows:
Detroit, ghost-gray, a frozen apparition.
You sense before you see the tire factory;
molten rubber can be smelled for blocks.

Your face, ghost-gray, a frozen apparition
glares back from the glass of the time clock,
throat blocked against the smell of molten rubber,
heat reddening the back of your neck.

"5:00 a.m." – your card stamped by the time clock,
you shuffle to your place in line;
heat flushes the back of your neck,
sweat bonds rubber to your pores.

You shuffle to your place in line,
nod toward the grimy man that you replace,
sweat bonds rubber to his pores,
your shoulders so much narrower than his.

You become the grimy man that you replace,
components uniform and interchangeable;
your muscles, smaller than the other men's,
still spend ten hours hoisting rubber cylinders.

Components uniform and interchangeable –
you strain to check for flaws in meager light.
After ten hours hoisting rubber cylinders,
the back screams and the eyes burn.

It's hard to check for flaws in the stain of light
cast by forty watts suspended overhead.
Back home, your eyes burning,
your mother points, wants to know, "What's wrong?"

Forty watt bulb swings bare above your head.
Marie comes to the shop floor, though you've begged her not to,
pointing at the foreman, "What's wrong with you?"
while the line men chuckle behind your back.

Marie on the shop floor; old wool coat begs
mending. She never flinches, facing the foreman.
Though the line men chuckle behind your back,
no one's ever stood up to him before.

You don't flinch as the foreman fires you.
Too late to slip once more behind a scarred wooden desk.
Monday finds you standing outside the gates at Ford,
skinny boy in man's work boots.

1937 - Marie

BENZEDRINE

Three sons kicked
through my womb
ever since
the third one
Frank, was born
I can't seem
to lose spare
tire hugs my
waist like raw
dough wide bulge
of my once
slender hips
my husband
Adolph dreams
as he eyes
firm asses
of young girls
on sunny
boulevards
me I'm all
used up breasts
slack empty
sacks never
enough dough
for silky
stockings new
dresses hair
grown straggly
thin my husband
he never comes
near Doctor
I want to be
thin when he
comes home make
him remember
a girl on
a sunlit
boulevard
waiting shadows

under my
eyes waiting
up for him
it's cold in
the shadows
Doctor those
pills the white
ones make me
forget my
hunger eat
away at my
bones hollow
my thoughts to
one thin tight
thread
that races
screaming through
the day Doctor
I want some more.

HOUSE AFIRE

1.
Here at last was warmth
enough to hold her
a thin vein of red
along the dim hallway
tendrils curling
orange and blue.

Faces spit from flames
and she grinned back
as curtains leapt
to lick the ceiling
glass panes burst
from their tidy frames.

2.
. . . they'd given her
the gas can at the filling
station no questions a woman
on foot flapping overcoat
revealing torn dingy
nightdress the attendant
flushed offered her a lift
she refused clutched
the metal spout against
her hip inhaling
its perfume careful
not to spill the long walk home . . .

3.
She set the parakeet free.
It perched, blinking, on its cage door
until she had to grab hold
carry it to the gaping window – its heart
hammered in her palm – throw it
to the sky. *Remember how to fly.*

4.
The refrigerator would not burn
though its smug face blackened
and the stove exploded
with a satisfying boom.

LOST CHRIST

How could Jesus ever find
me in these dull green
rooms where the smell of shit
is rubbed right into
the paint and splattered blood
is just another bright
pattern on the linoleum
thick with peeled skin
and the thin slop that spills
from our heaving throats Jesus
would have to hunt
among the wards crowded
with so many disciples –

       young girl with a crooked
       spine who carves butterflies
       into her blue-veined arms

       hag with red eyes
       who spits and masturbates
       all day with a plastic ashtray

       pregnant German who tries
       to strangle me, who swears
       I seduced her dead husband

       fat one who steals
       my meat, hides a crust
       of bread in her shoe for her lost dog

       bulldyke with broken
       teeth, whose punch split the doctor's
       jaw, who howls curses at the dark

– how could Jesus even find
his way inside, only men
in here are guards, they stalk
the night with snakes, Jesus
in a white uniform, thick-

soled boots and a halo
of keys, would he slip
the locks, search the throng
of sinners, attend their oozing
sores, would he change
us into fishes, would he
pick me out and choose
me like he did Magdalene?

1937 - Marie

PACK

They say they do this to help
calm us down but who can relax
strapped to a rubber pad

sometimes I think it's my own skin
chilled wet tightly wrapped around
stinging nerves I believe I must

be dead only a corpse could
be so cold and I can't move stiff
as a carcass my mouth

hollow my eyes open and close
the dead can't do that but see
nothing this dark place faint shadows

of shadows and the sheets crawl
over my bones they hold me no
one holds me here the plank

under my spine holds me rigid
as a coffin floor my jaw
chatters while mold creeps over damp

flesh furry and green time drips
somewhere beyond my hearing light
sickens falls from the sky

blood burns to a crystal ash don't
bother to yell they say we
won't come as if the dead could wail

—∿∿—

Ononharoia
("The upsetting of the brain")

*The main winter festival . . . [was performed when] . . . many people in the village
were sick. . . . bands of people who felt ill at ease [went] through the village
singing and shouting. These people entered all of the houses, where they
proceeded to upset furnishings . . . and toss firebrands about. Occasionally these
activities resulted in a house catching fire. The next day they returned and
announced that each of them had dreamed about something. The villagers were
called upon to guess the nature of these dreams and to present each person with
the object that had been revealed to him. When he was finally offered [the
object] he was looking for, he took it as a sign that the troubles that were threatening
him had been averted. . . . [Then] the participants went into the forest to cast out
their madness.*

— Bruce G. Trigger, *The Huron: Farmers of the North*

1.
Red snakes slide
through tunnels
in my head, drag
twisted muscle
from black cave
to black cave.
I hear dirt crunch
beneath their bellies,
hisses echo
always in my ears.

2.
Those of us with snakes
in our skulls race
through the village
at dusk; our feet
raise the red dust,
snake screams
in our raw throats.
We crash through your door,
shatter your pots,
set your rooms to blaze.

48

3.
Will you look at me
long enough to know
the content of my dream?
Stare into my red
gaze and offer
what will cure? Not
the pipe, crow's feather,
the skin of the doe.
Only the red bead
can ease my madness.

4.
Bead clenched
in my fist, I run
to the forest, sun
sparks the pines, glows
in white sky. I swallow
the bead, earth opens
to receive me, snakes
spill from my lips,
my eyes, slither
beneath the red crust.

DISCHARGE

The lawn had not recovered –
patches of scorched dirt edged
with blackened tufts that crumbled
into ash beneath her shoes.

The porch seemed suddenly
to heave and pitch as she labored
up the blistered wooden steps;
one blind hand fumbled

at the railing, then clutched
so tight the chipped paint slivered
in her palm. The door trembled, swung
askew, its threshold gaping

like a mouth to gobble her.
A mistake, a trick, the wrong
address! The man who gripped
her elbow was a liar –

she had no husband. Or if
she did, he dwelled forever
in a bottled cave of night,
where waterfalls of amber

spilled their sad, dark music.
The man beside her swore this was her home
but the small house – fresh paint, square
windows and rose-colored walls –

held nothing she remembered.
An unfamiliar ceiling loomed,
dusky as the sky above the Rouge
Plant, and the neat rectangles

spaced along the hallway framed
two boyish faces she could not recall,
although their eyes burned toward her.
Even her image in the silvered

mirror stared without recognition.
Only the tarnished bird cage
stirred her memory, suspended
in the corner from its metal

spine, the latched door, the empty
perch that swayed before her gaze.
That's when she turned and pushed
the screen door wide, moved with halting

steps into the early evening light,
then lumbered down the splintered stairs to drop
her body to the dirt and press
one cheek against charred spokes of grass.

ANNULMENT

Next time you see Irene
at work, six weeks after
that sticky night under
the basement stairs, she waits

by the time clock, whispers
hoarsely, "I need to talk
to you." She's not bleeding.
"I think something happened,

my father will kill me."
You redden to the roots
of your sandy hair. Your
mother thumps your skull, back

of her flattened hand.
"Marry her, Art," she demands.
Then you're standing before
sour priest – Irene's white dress

stretched across her belly,
your shoes too tight – slipping
a cheap gold band onto
her swollen finger. Fall

into her eyes but don't
recognize the stranger
who stares back. Two cramped rooms
over a dry goods shop.

You try to bring home treats,
a cut of meat, a pint
of ice cream – strawberry,
her favorite, though you

prefer rocky road – still
she ducks your kiss. Six hours
you fidget on a hard
bench at the hospital.

Somewhere a radio
broadcasts the Tigers' game.
They're winning, and a nurse
with tired eyes appears;

your son is stillborn, choked
by the cord. They won't let
you look, so imagine
the pulp of a sparrow

fallen from the nest. Back
home, Irene flutters from
room to room, always lighting
wherever you are not.

Across the stretch of sheets,
she turns her back. Months pass.
The priest is no less grim
as he undoes his spell –

the gold ring slipped from her
finger, vows unsworn –
erasing two cramped rooms,
song of sparrow at dawn.

PATERNITY

When bombs fall on Pearl Harbor,
the landscape shifts, our globe shrinks,
sons are called to duty. Next
morning finds you in line at
Navy Recruiting, where blue-
clad men refuse you because
of rotten teeth. *I never
planned to bite the enemy.*
Army is more forgiving;
just some routine paperwork,
certificate of birth. Marie
first claims to have lost it,
but at the sight of your hunched
shoulders, retrieves the folded

record from her jewelry
box. You snatch it, turn to leave
when she says, *Look at it, Art.*
The odd glitter in her eyes
as you unfold square after
square, page crumbling under your
touch, soft as the skin of an old
man. You stare without looking,
not sure what she wants you to
see. Her hand wavers as she points
Here, and lands on the line marked
"Father." Letters march across
your vision, don't spell what you
expect: name of the man whose

nearness makes you bristle, scent
of tobacco and gin, who
skulks through your nightmares clutching
a ribbon of belt, soft snake
that curls in your lap, then strikes.
The letters make a puzzle,
and your eyes plead questions. Your
mother lights a cigarette,
smoke blues the air, *I was married*

before, taps the form, *he
was a bartender.* She squares
her shoulders, ready to brawl,
her feet set wide. Black eyes spark,
diamonds in coal. *Adolph,*

*he's a good man, gave his name,
raised you like his own.* The page
blurs and swims; landscape shifts,
globe shrinks. You are not who you
thought. Like a curse removed, blood
free of the taint of him, his hands,
his name, his sauerkraut breath.

1943 - Detroit

WAR

The Nazi-controlled Vichy radio hailed
the Detroit riots as a "revolt" that would
spread to other cities, a reflection of "the
moral and social crisis in the United States . . .
the French people . . . realize the dangers . . .
inherent in the American aims of world
domination."

                    – Alfred McClung Lee, *Race Riot*

First day of summer, war time.
Throngs on Belle Isle cling to
the dimming light of weekend,
linger past sunset to catch
one last river breeze before
returning to cramped, hot rooms,
sleepless nights. Sailors, sweethearts,
loners, and families pack
picnic things, shake loose grass from
blankets, gather balls and sand
pails, begin slow trek across
bridge that spans from island to
city, Sunday to Monday,
into the waiting arms of
the assembly line.
                    A brawl
erupts; no one knows who starts
it, who jostled elbows, whose
eyes stared too long. The vast
migration from the withered
farmlands of Georgia,
Kentucky, the lure of war's
abundant crop of jobs, have led
thousands to this crossing – great-
grandsons of slaves and former
sharecroppers trade insults first,
then fists. When squad cars arrive
at ten-thirty, sirens squall,
melee spills from bridge onto

56

Jefferson Avenue, mob
five thousand strong.
                        A lit match
dropped in gasoline, Detroit
explodes. By midnight, rumors
swirl through a Colored nightclub
that white men stabbed a Colored
mother on Belle Isle, threw her
baby from bridge. Swing shift lets
out, workers hear that Negroes
raped young white girls swimming in
the river. The streets ignite –
cars stoned, streetcars set upon, white-
owned stores looted, vandalized,
Negro patrons beaten as
they leave the all-night Roxy
theater.
                Hospital cites
the injured coming in at
one per minute. Factory
workers yanked from cars, pummeled.
Gangs of young, white toughs hunt black
men, brandish knives, go after
colored schoolboys with baseball
bats, elderly Negroes chased,
bleed on sidewalks while police
look on. Cars are set on fire
on Woodward Avenue, charred
hulls left smoking in front
of shattered storefronts. Sniping
begins, bullets spit from gun
barrels, scorch a path through
viscera.
                Dearborn is miles
from the battleground. Adolph
watches embers glow from his
Chesterfield, shakes his head as
radio crackles news. Thinks
of his father's shoe store, once

proud on Woodward Avenue,
how he'd arrange the window
displays – small platforms, varied
elevations. Imagines
pumps scattered across pavement,
the shop in ruins. Marie
paces in the small bedroom,
recalls the day flames tongued its
dusky walls, sparks snapping like
conversation.
                    Those sparks speak
still, drowning the radio
voice, bright synapses flashing,
warming dark corners of her
brain. And Arthur pilots
his B-17, looping
above the unseen globe. Glow
of the instrument panel
comforts like a heartbeat;
engines' drone extinguishes
memory. He aims earthward
to sear Tunisian skies,
rain fire on North Africa.
Marie tosses in her sleep,
smiles, dreams a world set ablaze.

1943

P.O.W.

1. Arthur

All day you press your face
into ferns, hips flattened
to forest floor, the weight
of a felled tree trunk for
shelter. Some small relief:
to feel held in the grip
of earth after your long
tumble from sky. Hunker
into waiting; try to
ignore the damp seeping
into pant legs, bladder
straining full, as boredom
leaches the sting of fear.

Above you, shadows skulk;
you watch their guns tracking
a sudden flush of birds,
any creak of branches.
They must've found the smoking
wreckage of your B-17 –
"my lucky plane," you once
called it – and the slack ghost
parachute. A matter
of time till they find you.
Pray to a god discarded
years ago, but he can't
deliver you from this:

Alone, hunger scraping
your entrails, wings clattered
to dirt. You're stuck behind
enemy lines, dressed in
the wrong uniform, no
papers, no language,
no maps to guide you out.
God is as impotent
as ever, pathetic

like you, as the pale sun-
light begins to dim, air
grows colder, mist settles,
thickens the stand of trees.

Now you stagger upright,
swaying on the sprained left
ankle, flinch as your weight
compresses it. You turn
to face the dark open
mouths of Lugers, pointed
as the harsh syllables
spat from between clenched teeth.
A month ago you turned
twenty-two. Now your heart
shudders under aching
ribs as you slowly raise
your arms, stretch hands to sky.

2. Marie

Marie never receives the letter
from the U.S. Department of War.

She's back in Eloise. Chemicals
swilled from paper cups burn like tracers

in a black sky. Like you, she is locked
in a cell, bound to her rough cot at night.

She is always cold in her thin, stained
gown; coarse blanket barely covers her

white legs. Sleepless, she dreams to strangled
whispers of bored guards on the graveyard

shift, their listless words dissolved into
shards of noise, a language she can't speak,

their stories receding to a blank
horizon. Sometimes they'll let her smoke,

careful to keep matches from her reach;
other days she might catch a sharp kick

in the ribs, a cuff in the soft cage
of her skull. The doctors determine

that the letter is too disturbing,
so she still imagines you in flight,

a silver flash of wings over Germany,
as she slumps over her morning meal

of mush, or plucks loose threads from her sleeve.
It comforts her to see you flying.

Just as you imagine her at home,
padding the floors in her house slippers,

chain-smoking Lucky's over a cup
of reheated coffee. November's

pale sun leaks through the window.
Pot roast boils with potatoes in broth.

NOSE ART

What woman wouldn't swoon to see her name
red-lettered across the silver body
of a fighter jet? What woman wouldn't
open her womb to the man who'd stencil
those letters?
                Next thing you know, a toddler
and an infant, girl and boy. Now you're steeped
in diapers while your sobriquet soars
off without you – England and Germany,
Egypt, Libya.
                Some glyph of you preens in
exotic skyscapes while at home you scar
cigarette filters with blood red lips, skim
Photoplay, try to scrub sour milk scent
from your skin.
                And when your husband returns,
hero, handsome in captain's uniform,
stranger to his children, prowler in your
bed, you long to lay siege to his distant
peninsula.
                Instead, you surrender, scan
maps for escape routes, recalculate your
coordinates. Begin to rearrange
the fragile alphabet of loyalty.

JEFF

How can a little boy compete
with fighter planes? He's much too small,
too weak to hold his father's eye,
this man who streaks across the sky,
rains fire down on towns of sleeping
boys. He is always sleeping
when his father comes. He dreams a
tall man scowling by his bed, smells
starch and cigarettes and gin. Cold
gaze raining on his head, he wakes
to empty dark.
              Years later, he
will cruise the parks and alleyways,
the Castro bars. He'll favor chest
hair, weathered skin, thick-waisted men
who fire their hot rain into him.
When the virus spirals in his blood,
blitzing cells, he'll hunker in
his hospital bed and, dozing,
dream the man with silver wings,
vanishing tracer in the sky;
he, the flaming ruin below.

TRAITOR

What did Marie know of your nights
at the Officers' Club, post-War
England, American heroes
feasting on platters of prime rib,
blood rare, Beefeater's sparkling
over rocks, women in their best
dresses – hair pinned up, still rib-thin
from years of rations, hiding bad
teeth behind lipstick smiles, dancing
to "Take the A Train" – clung to their
Yank pilot like their last, best hope?

Marie knew this: her son was in
the War, handsome in uniform,
pressed and creased. She knew he flew planes;
recalled the movies, gray newsreels
showed giant silver birds birthing
fire on the enemy below,
black eggs dropping from split bellies,
cities erupting in flame. No
matter it was nineteen fifty-
three, peace negotiated, next
war brewing in South China Sea.

So when she saw Verda, your wife,
at the Top Hat on Michigan
Avenue, clinging to a thick-
skulled man in a business suit,
one high heel slipping down the rung
of the stool, Lucky Strikes cornered
in the ashtray, a coral smear
on the rim of a daiquiri
glass, jukebox playing "Fools Rush In,"
painted nails on a wide lapel,
laughter rising above the song,

Marie heard roaring overhead,
felt pavement shudder, a shadow
of metal sweep cool across her
cheek before the sky went black, flares
on the horizon, smell of soot,
blood drenched into ground. Her belly
split open; she longed for black eggs
to detonate, reduce to ash
this enemy stronghold. Her son
was in the war, a traitor too
near. What could she do but tell you?

VIXEN

Crazy like a fox
he always said when
he told the story,
how she'd started
to go off again,
his phrase for how
she'd stay in bed all
day, striking matches,
tossing them in air,
watch them fall, blazing
snowflakes, scorch marks
on the mattress,
on her white legs,
mouth full of Jesus
and damnation, eyes
burning through him, staring
down the devil, room
reeking of sulfur, floor
littered with spent
matchsticks curled as
blackened worms, fingers
barbed when he tried
to calm her down

She might be crazy
he'd allow *but, oh, she's*
cunning when he bundled
her into the old
Chevy for the trip back
to Eloise, she stretched
her torso from the gaping
window, shrilled her plight
to the startled sidewalk,
a transitory siren, hurtling
past, snaring the attention
of the cops on the beat
who could not resist
pursuit, sirens wailing,
and her story: *kidnapped*

by this creep, a stranger
she: hair wild, no shoes,
house dress askew; he:
overalls muddy, boots
caked with grime, scratch
marks drilled into his
cheeks, then the handcuffs
biting his wrists

Listen, she's my wife
he pleaded, but by that time
she was calm, eyes wily,
He's nuts! I never saw him
in my life, her grin sly as they
dragged him off to lock-up, stale
smoke and sweat, urine soaked
into each corner of the cell,
all night shouts and curses
invaded his fitful dreams,
Marie rutting in a bed of flame,
when reached her doctor verified
his story, *"Sorry, buddy,"*
the police released him
to a used-up night, back
home he found her curled
on the sofa, dozing, naked,
cigarette still glowing
in the ashtray perched atop
her belly, white track of stretch marks
from her three grown boys, TV
flickering blue against
the dark walls of her lair.

1957 - Marie

BINGO

Black as buttons, plastic
  markers dot my card, round,
  flat wafers blot out numbers;
  impure Host, they just can't guarantee
  my chances for salvation

I pray the alphabet, "B" for my boys,
  two at home and the one left
  behind, the busted promise
  of numbers never called, broken
  hopes of an ignorant girl

Nowadays I play the Specials –
  Goal Post, Nine Pack, Indian
  Sign; I look for order in
  the random calls, wait for blanks
  to fill, some pattern to emerge

Gains never outweigh losses;
  it's true in every game – no
  matter that I bow my head before
  these numbers, beg God to bless
  my boys and my bughouse brain

Obedient, I hear each call and press
  another marker down, an eye
  that never blinks, a wafer
  melting on my tongue; God, bring me luck
  as I go gambling with ghosts

KINDLE

When Art brought her over to the house – his
new wife, his fourth, but who am I to talk? –
I liked her. Taller than he was, even
without high heels. Skinny, wore her clothes like
a model. Dark hair, dark eyes – exotic.
"You've got yourself a good one," I told him,
but it was her little girl I really
noticed; she was just five. Not used to dogs,
she hung back, fearful, till the old collie
nuzzled her, tail wagging. Then she sat, hands
plunged into the dog's thick fur, waited while
we had a drink, maybe two. More still
than any kid I'd ever seen, watching
everything; she didn't miss a trick.

I wasn't close to my own granddaughter;
not her fault I couldn't stand her mom. When
Art divorced her, he let go his daughter,
his son. Children are like cinders; they scar
us and we don't hold on. Released, they rise
into the night sky, pass from sight. When I met
Art's stepdaughter, a spark ignited, leapt
across the breach of time from her eyes to
mine; this girl, too, was born to burn. *Careful,
when I think this way, they lock me up.* Eyes
serious, hazel; dishwater blonde; plump
belly strained seams of her green cotton dress.
This child looked nothing like her mom. She could
belong to anyone. She could be mine.

BOOK TWO

1957 - 2000

IDOL

My mother had never heard
of Neil Sedaka,
was puzzled when,
lounging by the hotel pool,
the redhead on the next chaise
swooned. Spring break. 1957.
Although the same age
as the pony-tailed coed,
my mother had dropped
the skein that bound her
to her generation, threads
of movie stars and pop tunes,
dance steps and the latest styles.

A college drop-out, two years
married to the high school
sweetheart who'd turned mean
before the wedding cake
was sliced, exiled at twenty-three
to a salt box house in rural, Gulf Coast
Florida, the only radio station
preaching Jesus, her days were chock
with formula and shit-streaked diapers,
grime of shabby rooms, palm-sized
spiders in the bath, my father
coming home swinging or
not coming home at all.

Those muggy nights she'd rock
me, try to remember her life,
the precise blue of an October
day in Michigan, the high school
yearbook that proclaimed her,
"A Greek Goddess," her hair now
limp with humidity, sweat
tinged with cigarettes, miles
from nowhere on a dirt road,
no car. She'd try to recite
the Periodic Table of Elements,

– hydrogen, helium, lithium –
a halting lullaby;

she'd once majored in chemistry.
Now on the threshold of her first
divorce, her mother had sent her money
for a Miami Beach vacation
before she left the state behind
for good. She wanted sun to bake
the hurt out, help her to feel young
once more. The commotion
at the lifeguard stand
confused her. "There he IS!"
the redhead pointed, squealed.
My mother squinted in the light
and wondered, "Who?"

RED BALLOONS

My mother disappeared each morning
dressed in secretary's skirt and sweater
glamorous in high heels, left me yearning

for her red lips, Woodhue cologne, fettered
to my fretful grandma, long days
spent eating sweet rolls, growing fatter

watching "Edge of Night," "Queen for a Day."
Age three, I'd learned to track the sweep of time
anticipate the crunch of her wheels on driveway.

I'd want to hug her with sticky hands, climb
into her lap, inhale the scent
of Marlboros and black coffee, grime

of carbon on her fingertips, content
to sit beside her in the big green chair,
but she was already leaving again. I'd resent

the man who waited at the door, hair
slicked back, convertible parked at curb.
I'd ball my fists; how could she prefer

his company to mine? Sometimes I'd disturb
their swift departure, setting up a wail
so shrill it could be heard

until that open car would fishtail
past the corner. Grandma lulled me to bed,
with chocolate ice cream and a fairytale,

still I'd will myself awake, clutching the plaid
blanket in my crib, until I heard my mother
tiptoe in, undress in darkness, sigh and spread

her weary body on the mattress, not bother
to kiss me good night. I was four
that Halloween, first time my grandfather

took me trick-or-treating. I wore
the long skirt of a gypsy, big hoop
earrings, lipstick lifted from my mother's drawer.

After I'd hauled home my pillowcase loot,
my mother's date arrived. A new one, he brought
me a bouquet of red balloons, Baby Ruth

bars for her. Grandma scowled at the sight
of him – three times married, a life strewn
with wreckage – but I forgot

to cry as my mother left, humming a jukebox tune,
escaping through the door he held open.
I tugged the string of a balloon.

He was the only one who'd ever spoken
to me; the courtship left my cheeks burning,
my face reflected round in red stretched skin.

THE ANNIVERSARY WALTZ

Oh, how we danced on the night we were wed . . .
— "The Anniversary Waltz"
by Al Dubin and Dave Franklin

I didn't understand
harsh voices behind closed
doors, my mother's reddened
eyes, why grandma wouldn't
dress me or curl my hair
this special morning when
I would be Flower Girl.
Tomorrow my birthday;
I'd be five.
              Long car ride,
dusty road to no place
I'd been – not the Chinese
laundry or grocery
store, not the lunch counter
where Stan and Lydia
served hot fudge sundaes with
chopped nuts in chrome dishes
lined with white paper cones,
not Beulah's dress shop where
my beautiful mother
coveted the latest
styles on secretary's
pay, not church where grandma
searched the lawn for four-leaf
clovers.
        A '53
two-tone Chevy drove us
past the borders of my
known world, sun glancing off
hood and windshield, no air
moving in the back seat
where my dress wrinkled, legs
stuck to vinyl. Blue wreaths
of smoke bloomed from glowing

ends of Marlboros, my
mother's tears glistening
behind their veil. Driver
never stopped talking, lilt
in his voice to soothe her,
this man who would be my
father now; once he'd brought
me red balloons – that's all
I knew of fathers.

                    But
I knew we were doing
it wrong, not like weddings
I'd watched on grandma's soaps,
"Edge of Night," "As the World
Turns." I kept wondering
when white dress would appear,
bright blossoms woven through
hair. The JP's chamber
was dusty beige and cramped,
empty but for us, terse
Justice of the Peace, his
bored wife, and Margaret,
my mother's friend from work,
her boyfriend Buddy. I
begged to wait till grandma
got there, but they said no.
There were no flowers for
me to hold, no "Here Comes
the Bride." The whole thing took
ten minutes: the ring, quick
kiss, then pile back into
car. Afternoon fading
to summer evening,
we were quiet the whole
drive home.

A pizza joint
for the nuptial dinner,
red-checked tablecloths,
scent of tomato sauce
and garlic. Drinks ordered,
perhaps a toast. I sucked
ice water, unconsoled.
Until I spied the juke
box – blue neon glowed like
heaven – begged a nickel,
and scanned the list of tunes
for the perfect song. *Oh,
how we danced on the night
we were wed.* The grownups
clinked cocktails; I found more
coins, filled the moment with
music. Today my life
had changed forever. I
deserved a ritual.

MY TWO GRANDMOTHERS

1. Elsba

She recited long poems from memory
as we walked through her quiet neighborhood,
stopping for a bag of butter cookies
from the bakery, searching the wide green
lawns that ringed the Presbyterian church
for four-leaf clover (never found.) She sang
hymns from her childhood, one about pansies,
their cheery faces, another praising
the light of a tiny star. She, who read
to me each night until her voice was raw,
who wove the threads of story through my dreams.
Her lap was softer than my mother's; we'd
sit watching "Edge of Night," nose pressed against
her shoulder, inhaling her scented powder.

2. Marie

Because my first grandmother disapproved
my mother's second marriage to a man
three times divorced, I was placed into his
mother's care. She wore cheap housedresses, gray
strings of hair hung limp to jaw line, nylon
stockings rolled to her ankles. A yellowed
ivory cigarette holder bloomed
perennial between her lips, one always
lit, smoke curling heavenward. Her voice held
a snarl, cracked glass on metal shards, laughter
rasping behind blackened, broken teeth,
and she cursed inventively. She stayed in bed
all day while I filched chocolate for my lunch;
nights we caught cabs out to the bingo hall.

BIPOLAR

1. Tootsie

Already an old dog when I first met
my grandmother, Tootsie wanted nothing
more than to doze on the worn rag rug, find
a patch of sun to warm her russet coat,
close milky eyes and dream through her remaining
days. Gentle, she withstood with weary
patience my attempts at play, hobbled
to retrieve the rubber ball without a snarl,
forbore the curious fingers that probed
her ears and pulled her tail. I snuck dark squares
of Hershey's from my grandmother's kitchen,
made the collie beg as I crooned a song
I'd learned from my new stepfather: *Toot-toot*
Tootsie, don't cry, Toot-toot-Tootsie, bye-bye . . .

2. Sparky

Scarcely bigger than a big city rat,
my grandmother's new Chihuahua had fierce
black eyes that shone like polished onyx struck
with fire. Scrawny, he trembled constantly
as if in permanent indignation.
Toe nails clicked a nervous beat as he paced
the shabby rooms of her small house. His high-
pitched yelp was raw, sharp as the little teeth
bared with a low growl. One day he leapt three
feet to bite my stepfather's behind, missed
the skin but grabbed a mouthful of brown work
pants. He would not let go, and hung there, paws
scrabbling in air, while my grandmother
chortled her approval, *The little shit.*

1959 ~ Terry

DRIVE-IN

The toy Drive-in Movie was my favorite
Christmas present the year I was five: squat
plastic snack bar in caution yellow snapped
into molded blacktop where small cars parked;
toy projector shone a beam of light at
the white screen; tiny replicas of hot
dogs and popcorn bags, soda cups – easy
pieces to lose. First Christmas with my new
stepfather, rundown downtown apartment
where I was not allowed to go outside.
One bedroom; each night at eight they'd tuck me
into bed, awaken me past midnight
to complete my sleep on rough upholstered
sofa. Same year my mother and I came
home from shopping to find him hanging out
the window, legs dangling from sill, trying
to stencil Glasswax snowflakes on eighteenth-
story panes. I loved the Drive-in Movie,
though it never worked right: could never make
pictures flicker on the screen, only bare
light boring into empty field of white.

I was playing on the carpet, that late
December afternoon he first summoned
me into the bathroom, voice coaxing through
crack of the almost-closed door. I left cars
on their plastic lot, miniature snacks
littering their path. I entered into
a world of steam; it fogged the air, clouding
mirrors, leaving a film of tiny drops
on porcelain. It shrouded my naked
stepfather, dumb smile on his lips. Each sound
magnified – click of my school shoes on tile,
faucet drips against water's skin – here
in this small room with locked doors. Bubbles brimmed
at the tub's edge; he scooped up a handful,
crooned, "Come here." I wasn't afraid; this man
was my father now, he wanted to play.
I perched on the rim, still in my little

dress, plunged my hands into soapy brine, scrubbed
his shoulders like he told me, kneaded the round
moons of his butt, giggled at how he said
"butt," knowing grandma would disapprove.

A game, he said. I followed directions,
fished deeper, found the soft snake that grew stiff
in my grasp, wagged at me like a taunting
finger. He called it "he" with affection,
like a favorite doll he was willing
to share. Because he chuckled, I laughed too,
pushing loose flesh back and forth; like magic
it swelled in my hand until he shuddered
and groaned, spilled milk into my palm. Then I
didn't know whether to smile, the moment
deflating, water grown tepid. I left
him alone to towel dry, slipping back
to my Drive-in Movie, the projector's
faint hiss of air, the glare of its blind eye.

GROWN UP

Even though my mother was a grown up –
big purse, high heels, lipstick ("Cherries in the
Snow") – I could see six-year-old Ruthie
anytime she told this story: Christmas
during the Depression, when all she and
her sister got for presents was one
orange a piece. "Not even paper dolls,"
her voice would quaver, as if *I'd* handed
her the lump of coal. Perched on a corner
of my bed, smartly dressed for work, sweater
and skirt, hair blonded from the beauty shop –
this image would recede, replaced by dark-
eyed child too skinny for her sister's hand-
me-downs, thick stockings fallen, bunched around
her ankles. She stares into snowdrifts, eyes
burning. Too stung for gratitude, too guilty
to cry. Hand grips the fruit in disbelief,
crushed, soured as juice stinging her curled palm.

1960 ~ Arthur

SLAMMER

Every man in jail is innocent
and my stepfather no exception:
good citizen, he'd made that alimony payment,

bitch ex-wife was gifted at deception.
The skinny deputy had heard it all before;
gun at hip, he'd brook no interruption

of his duty: flashed his keys, unlocked the door
to the dingy, white-washed holding cell,
muttered, "McCarthy, meet McCarthy – *he's* in for

murder." The seated prisoner clutched a dirty towel
to the bleeding knife-wound in his shoulder;
his sweat-soaked tee shirt offered up the smell

of stale whiskey. Bruised, hung-over, he was ruder
than the guard; "Goddamn," he swore
in greeting, then crushed the glowing cinder

of his cigarette against the concrete floor.
My stepfather poked the lumpy cot. "That's funny, huh? Us
having the same name – say, what's your

first?" "Richard," the man spat, contemptuous.
"Arthur, but call me Mac," my stepfather reached out a hand
to shake. It hovered in the air, conspicuous,

unwelcome, till it fell back. The weight of silence spanned
the too-bright night, bare bulb never dimmed, time
crawled like water bugs across the filthy washstand.

Past midnight, Richard growled, "Ever been in jail before, done time?"
My stepfather shrugged: a German prison camp, the war,
years later, the brig, the Air Force kicked him out. His crime –

messin' with a sergeant's wife. Richard nodded, "Broads are
nothin' but trouble." No stranger to confinement,
he'd been in and out of lock-ups all his life. "Stole a car,

a few stick-ups, nothin' like this – this guy was an accident,
and now I'm goin' to prison; they'll throw away the key."
His forehead creased, eyes seemed to focus on a distant

point, then he suddenly demanded, "When's your birthday?"
"October 7, 1921," was the answer my stepfather
gave, and the convict's snarl grew gentle with dismay.

"My dad always used to say I had a brother,
name of Arthur, born October seventh, two
years before me. I was still in diapers when my mother

split. Dad told me how she packed her bags and left her ring, took you
but not me. He said her name's Marie; don't know what her last
name is now. I waited years, she never came back. I got a few

pictures, but that's it." Then the murderer stood, embraced
his cellmate, his dumbstruck sibling, long-lost kin.
Morning sundered them: my mother arrived with bail; Richard faced

a day-long transport, manacled, in leg irons, to state prison.
Emerging from jail, my stepfather must have found the sunlight
shattering, its fraudulent distinction

between bright and shadow, the fractured fiction of his life.
When he went to see his mother, to demand once more the story of his
    origin,
her ivory cigarette holder trembled as if his words would smite

her; she begged Jesus to forgive her sin,
and then she told her tale. But was it truth or just one more convenient
lie? He never knew. He never saw his brother again.

WITNESS

What I remember is the rain:
a frenzied beat against the roof of the car,
the storm closing over us like a shroud,
windshield fogged with our breath.

Frenzy beating on the car roof –
my mother and I in the back seat,
fogging the windshield with our breath
as I clutched her cold hand in mine.

I sat with my mother in the back seat
of my stepfather's battered black Cadillac
clutching her cold hand in mine
as we waited, idling, in silence.

In my stepfather's battered black Cadillac,
filled with the blue smoke of cigarettes,
we waited, idling, in silence
outside the state hospital for the insane.

The air was smoky with cigarettes,
fear soured my taste buds, iron on my tongue.
Into the state hospital for the insane
my grandmother was dragged, howling.

Did she taste fear, like iron, on her tongue,
or brackish cunning, plotting her escape,
as she was dragged, howling "Jesus!"
one arm gripped by her husband, the other by her son?

Certainly my grandmother had plotted an escape
but, wedged between driver and passenger
– one her husband, the other her son –
she had no chance to reach the doors.

Wedged between driver and passenger,
she never stopped cursing as they pulled her from the car.
I couldn't see them once they reached the doors
of the mist-cloaked building into which she disappeared.

She'd never stopped cursing that whole time in the car.
My mother murmured, "Don't think of her this way."
Once she disappeared inside that mist-cloaked building,
only four of us could make the journey home

My mother said, "Don't think of her this way,"
as if I could erase what I had witnessed.
All four of us were quiet on the ride home,
just the maddening slap of the wipers.

Silence, erasing everything we'd witnessed,
closed over us like a storm-drenched shroud.
That maddening ictus of the wipers:
what I remember is the rain.

1962 - Marie

INTAKE

Another doctor with his pad
of paper, manila folder,
another priest in a white coat.
He knows she's sinned. Already he's
consigned her soul to Hell's cleansing
furnace. Still, he wants confession,
and he will scratch a record of
her crimes onto smooth lined pages,
then prescribe a dose of lightning
to her brain, charred benediction.

That bolt that splits the night sky in
her swollen head, leaves the landscape
emptied, drained as a cracked hourglass,
trees and houses reduced to ash,
muffled birdsong in burnt daylight.
Their scorching strikes have robbed her of
her children's names, the recipe
for pot roast, the grace to foxtrot.
She can no longer sniff the scent
of roses blooming by her porch.

But all their flash and fire have not
erased the thing that stalks her, length
of pink, unweathered meat that bobs
and wags inside her waking dreams.
She could never tell this man, his
polished wingtips, manicured hands,
about the grinning penis, its
threats, its mocking song. Scolding
like a stubby finger when she tries
to sleep or shuts her eyes to pray.

ELECTROSHOCK

The scrubby elm is struck
a sudden bolt
whitens the smoky sky
branches flare like candelabra
roots curl to claw

No

The elm, uprooted
crashes to earth
bark scratches the dust
leaves blistered
scarred trunk trussed with rope

No

The trunk lies on a plank
table draped in white sheets
straps of leather bind
its girth and outstretched limbs
its branches shorn

No

Doctors grab rigid limbs
poke jumbled roots
sparks rise from every hollow
smell of scorch
and wood gone rotten

No

A woman lived in the tree
bark sealed her like skin
lightning burnt to heartwood
charred the ground beneath
no mushrooms sprout in its blackened shade

———

Awataerohi

During this ceremony, some curers warmed their hands
by rubbing or holding red-hot coals and then placed their
heated hands on the part of the patient's body that was diseased.
. . . other[s] . . . put hot stones in their mouths and made wild-animal
noises in the ill person's ear.
   The Wendat believed Awataerohi was particularly effective
in curing many ailments, and it was therefore frequently prescribed
by their curers.

                         — Nancy Bonvillain, *The Huron*

A pallet of beaver
pelts soften the dirt,
my ravaged body
stretched on the floor
of the curer's house.

Sickness stalks me
like a silver wolf,
red stain seeping into snow.
Firelight licks my cheek;
the curer crouches beside.

I stare at his palms,
lines seared away,
field of blisters
pink withered brown
crackling to the touch.

Once more he plucks
live coals for me, pads
of his fingers blacken, ooze,
into his body he takes
fire, gives it back to me.

And how his tongue
reddens, swell as
stones smolder there,
hot breath in my ear,
his howls track the wolf.

His hands scorch
as they hover above me,
ease the hard lump
in my chest, ache that can
only be burnt out.

1962 ~ Terry

STEPSISTER

Brunette with a bubble cut,
sixteen when she came to live
in our rented bungalow
in Allen Park, ward of the court,
her father's house the last stop
before juvenile detention.
My mother quit her job to give
"parental supervision," that year
the only time in all my growing up
that I'd come home to find her
there, spreading butter on saltines,
spooning applesauce from a jar.
Judy got the spare room
and my record player, but I didn't
mind: I was gaining a sister.
Eight years old, I prayed we'd be close.

She wasn't up for it, tough girl
who'd already swigged from the mug
of the grown-up world, taste
of cigarettes familiar on her tongue.
spine remolded in a bar-stool
sway, thighs accustomed to the weight
of older men, their wives safe at home.
She'd journeyed far beyond the realm
of movie dates and curfew, yearbooks
and the prom, the yearning
confidences of a mongrel sibling.
Her father had flown away
when she was just a small girl,
her upturned hand waving as the metal
bird was swallowed into sky. Grounded, Judy
knew that family couldn't save her now.

I was less sure. I loved her tight
skirts, scuffed black flats, the snarl
of her full lips. I daydreamed
to the music that spun under
her closed door: *I don't wanna*

say good-bye for the summer . . .
I longed to be invited in, perch
on the edge of her bed, study
the blue indifference of her eyes.
That day she asked me to walk
with her, I wanted her to take
my hand as we ambled along cracked
sidewalks past cramped houses
where aging Chevy's sprawled
on weedy lawns and tar steamed
and bubbled on unpaved gravel.

She led me farther than I was allowed
to go by myself, down past where
our street ended in an unhealed gash,
sliced in two by the half-built Southfield
freeway. I stared deep into the gouge;
red dust billowed from the mouths
of metal dinosaurs that chomped
and choked, then spit. A sign warned,
"CONSTRUCTION SITE. KEEP OUT" and I restrained
the index finger that ached to point it out
as Judy's long legs swung over the chain
barricade. She sauntered down the dirt
incline into the pit, into the hollowed
earth, and I scrambled after her,
grit caking my feet, scraping under
the straps of my once-white sandals.

At the bottom was a man, shirtless,
skin burnt the same red as the earth
walls thrusting up on both sides of us,
bare and raw all the way to where
jeans rode low on his waist. He grinned
to see her, "Well, hell-o," blue eyes
brightened against his florid cheeks,
as his boots climbed the grade. I waited
a long time under the glare of sky,
shifting one foot to the other,

soles stamping imprints in the dirt,
as they shared a cigarette,
murmured a language I didn't know,
yet somehow knew was the language
of sex. I felt ashamed of my damp
armpits, sweat pooling between my thighs.

Blown grit prickled my legs, white sun
gripped too tight. He kept twisting
the gold band on his finger; she
had stretched her tank top's neckline
down, baring more of her freckled chest.
"Tonight then?" I heard him say,
till she cut eyes in my direction,
shushing him. Her next words came
so low I could not hear them; still,
I knew she'd made a plan. The secret
thrilled under my scalp; this was what
sisters shared. Yet she never glanced
at me, her alibi, as we climbed up
to the street, strolled home under mapled
shade, low tune in the back of her throat,
step jaunty with promise.

FIRST MENSTRUATION, 11TH BIRTHDAY

that long august afternoon
time slow-baking
my birthday, but without candles
grandmother all day in bed
I wander with the dogs
room to cluttered room

TV in its corner – a
closed window; no
breeze inflects the crawling hours
my hair stinks of cigarette
air; mother won't come for
me till six o'clock

Tootsie, Sparky and I lunch
on chocolate
slab of molded Hershey's squares kept
solid in the Frigidaire
we scarf them all; ache grinds
at my low belly

sun flags, sky grays, thickens; as
the waning day
grows sadder, I chafe within
my swollen body, vessel
in which I've crouched, hiding
now I'm spilling out

some unfamiliar fullness
I can't contain
seeping into the cramped yard, drab
hushed rooms, disrupting the dreams
of my drugged grandmother
I huddle, rock, but

can't hold back; only later
do I find blood –
sticky icing smeared on cake-white
thighs – I let the dogs lick my
fingers until mom's car
crunches in the drive

ADVICE

I wasn't expecting
sharp raps at the back door
as I sat lazing over
Lipton tea and Pillsbury
biscuits, summer I turned
twelve, home alone and bored,
summer my stepfather
left us, shacked up with his
girlfriend and her kid.
I was still in pajamas

long day looming – wash dishes,
empty ashtrays, make beds,
work crossword puzzle, then
prowl the stores of Grandland
Shopping Center: browse racks
of paperbacks at Cunningham's
Drugs, treat myself to a hot
fudge creme puff at Sander's
Candies, flip through greeting
cards in the potpourri'd air

of Holiday Card Shoppe,
cruise make-up counters, record
bins at Kresge's five-and-dime,
visit the parakeets,
poke fingers through slim bars,
listen to their fretful
song, or the overcrowded
turtles, scrabbling across
each other's shells in their
glass prison. Or troll aisles

in the supermarket,
mesmerized by rows of cake
mixes, cookies and bagged
candy, trancing myself
on calm symmetry of
confection – in these ways

I tried to fill the stretch
of hours until my mother
came home from work. Sometimes she
stopped off at the park to sit

on swings and cry for her
second failed marriage. Each
day her arms grew thinner,
no bigger around than
branches of young trees, eyes
hollowed out. I would mix
martinis, potent with clear
gin, cook dinner – pork chops
or tuna casserole – coax
her to eat, bite after

trembling bite. She'd fall asleep
weeping in my arms. The knock
startled me. I wasn't
allowed to let anyone
in the house while my mother
was at work, but surely
this did not include my
grandmother, who stood squat
behind the screen, fierce grin
on her face, and brayed, "Hello,

Terry," with her cigarette
laugh. How had she gotten there,
no evidence of Adolph
idling curbside? I'd
never seen her drive – even
when she took me to Bingo
when I was little, we
always called a Yellow Cab.
Now she sat in the pink
kitchen, hair gray and thin, cropped

square at the chin, her teeth
like an old graveyard, some stones
blackened, others fallen, some
chipped away. Cheap housedress
hung to her bare shins, white
ankle socks buffered feet
from moccasins, offending
my twelve-year-old's fashion
propriety. "Where's Art?"
she demanded, seemed not

to know her son no longer
lived here. I shrugged, "At work,
I guess" – not my job to tell.
The wall clock beat relentless
time behind the whispered hum
of the refrigerator.
Her cheek twitched, never-ending
series of small grimaces.
"From shock treatments," my mother
had explained, "she can't help it."

Still she made me nervous,
eyes black as jet, too bright,
and how they seized me, helpless
as a parakeet snatched up
by a giant hand, wings
pinned, claws treading air,
and my lips invented
an excuse, a phantom
date to meet my friend Denise.
I tried to sound sorry

for this interruption;
my grandmother ignored
it, began to talk about
the powers of color: "Red
makes you strong, you can beat
the crap out of anyone

who tries to mess with you.
Yellow keeps you scared – don't
wear that piss color." I thought
she might continue through

the spectrum, but her tongue
leapt to another topic.
She had rules for everything,
code strict as Catholic
doctrine: the proper day
of the week on which to wash
laundry, the right time of night
to bathe, that one might eat
apples in July, never
June, though one might have gravy.

Her eyes never let go
of me. I squirmed in yellow
pajamas, chubby breasts
budding through thin cotton,
feet bare on linoleum.
I shifted from left to right,
beseeched the clock's face
as if its measures could save
me. "My friend, she's waiting,"
I reminded her, convinced

for a moment that Denise
was standing on the corner
of Grand River and Greenfield
to meet my bus, annoyed
at my lateness. "Is your friend
older?" my grandmother
inquired, then launched into
a new stream of protocol,
an elaborate dance
of human interchange:

"If she's older, she has
to walk on the outside
when you go down the street
with her. But – wait – are you
taller? Then you oughta
go on the outside . . ." She leaned
close enough that I could smell
her musty breath, feel the spray
of her spittle on my
cheek. Urgent that I learn

each tenet, observe them
devoutly, as if this faith
might keep me from some harm
she could not name. In the end
it wasn't my feigned protests
that silenced her; rather
she wound down like a music
box, its spring uncoiled, breath
expended in a sigh.
She fell back in the kitchen

chair, eyelids blinking, unsure
perhaps of where she was now,
or what gawky girl stood
guard, misery melting
her raw features. Then she heaved
her body to standing,
lumbered out the back door,
and disappeared into
the June afternoon, mission
accomplished, advice dispensed.

RIOT SONNETS

There had always been the fear . . .
that if a riot erupted in Detroit,
it would be one of massive proportions.

— Hubert G. Locke, *The Detroit Riot of 1967*

Sunday, July 23
1.

Saturday night bleeds into Sunday; heat
squeezes the street in its dense grip. Can't sleep,
nerves razored, sidewalks buzzing with bloods. Two
a.m., Vice raids the blind pig on Twelfth Street –
this shit keeps happenin – and bottles rain
on retreating cop cars. This is release,
and it flows sweeter when muscles strain to
hurl trash cans through store windows; glass spills like
diamonds to cement. Then the snatching –
a boogaloo of color TV's, air
conditioners. Little kids, old ladies,
moms in halter tops and hair curlers, white
folks – *like a muthafuckin carnival* –
four p.m. before the first fire is set.

2.

No money for vacation, so we spent
the weekend in Lansing, my mother and
I, baby-oiled at the pool, pampered in
the bland respite of Holiday Inn, low
back of her bathing suit exposing
the knobs of her spine, so thin now since my
stepfather's defection. In dark, quiet
restaurants she mourned betrayal, while I –
twelve-year-old Freud with bangs – spoon-fed comfort
and gin. Both sunburned, we drove home past dark
on Sunday night, oblivious to news,
marveling at sparse traffic. She slept that
night, skin flushed against white sheets, while I paced,
relieved I'd kept her safe another day.

Monday, July 24
3.

Flames mesmerize; the first golden crackle
spreads like liquid. Gasoline in a rag-
stopped bottle, spark at the end of a strong
arm, aimed at an open window, tinder
dry roof. The whole block is burning: beauty
salon where Sistah Ella braids the corn
rows, corner bar where James Brown wails all day,
shoe store where moms put a dollar a week
toward paying off their kids' new school shoes.
Reverend pleads *Why burn down yo own street?*
but fire licks the soul, a new baptism.
Smoke plumes scorch the air, extend their reach; white
houses cringe and tremble. Thick ash drifts
to pavement like black snow. *Amazing grace.*

4.

I brewed tea with milk, spread jam on buttered
biscuits, began the crossword puzzle in
the *Free Press* when my mother called from work.
They were sending her home, she told me, boss
amazed that she'd come in; didn't she know
Detroit was burning? We'd avoided news,
cocooned inside our own raw troubles, no
idea we'd violated curfew
driving home the night before. *That must
be why there was no traffic.* Five miles from
our house, stores were being looted, all gas
stations ordered closed. At my stepfather's
garage at the end of our street, the doors
were padlocked, Shell sign no longer turning.

5.

Police Log, July 24, 1967 11 p.m.-Midnight

[11:07] Livernois north of Grand River; sniper
cornered, may be in church tower. [11:12] St. Jean
north of Warren; fire house under heavy
fire. [11:30] St. Jean-Mack; firehall besieged, almost
out of ammo. [11:35] St. Jean-Mack; firehall under
attack. [11:37] Firing at [precinct] number
seven from across the street. [11:41] Gratiot-
Grandy, Mt. Elliott-Sylvester; both
firehalls pinned down by snipers. Crane-Brinkett;
fire at firehall. [11:45] Mack-St. Clair; sniper fire.
Jefferson-St. Jean; firing at rear of
fifth precinct – all officers go in front
door. [11:46] Gratiot-Mack; officer and National
Guard shot. [11:47] Southeastern Command Post under
fire. [11:48] Sniper fire on fire stations Gratiot–
Grandy, Mt. Elliott-Sylvester. [11:50]
Heavy sniper fire at Eastern High School
Command Post. [11:51] Mack-St. Jean; fireman shot, need
car in hurry. [11:52] Two wagons at number
seven, officers shot. [11:56] Mack-St. Jean, heavy
fire. [12 M] Davison–Mt. Elliott; firehouse,
heavy fire. Gratiot–Mack; small war, need help.

Tuesday, July 25
6.

Grit-gray rooftops rise above the city's
blistered heart, arteries drained; streets below
stretch empty, spokes in a broken wheel. Air
cool this time of day, sun not yet begun
to drag itself up through layers of ash;
sirens for the moment stilled, replaced
by songs of birds – *Crazy fuckers*. He shakes
his head clear of smoke and sleeplessness. Black
metal sawed-off shotgun rests light against
the hip, bullets fed tenderly. Scattered
underfoot, spent casings like dried cocoons
after butterflies have gone – *Grandpap used
to show me those*. Below, squad car crawls
the pavement. He crouches, takes aim, squeezes.

7.

My mother wanted me to stay inside
but that was stupid; no riots came to
our neighborhood, though I prayed they would. I
wanted our street to combust – smug houses,
tidy brick, well tended lawns charred. Buick's
blackened carcass; gin bottles exploded.
I longed for a healing flame to blister
my walls of skin, anneal my festering
heart. Bolting the door only locked terror
in. *I can't be cooped up here*, I whined till
she let me go – *Just to the corner; come
right back, do you hear?* That's when I saw tanks
rumbling down Grand River Avenue,
like TV pictures of Viet Nam.

Wednesday, July 26
8.

He'd done his tour in 'Nam, made it back from
that hellhole jungle in one piece; figured
the Guard was an easy way to pick up
extra cash, plus catch up with some buddies
once a month. Never dreamed he'd drive a tank
through an American city, streets on
fire, sniper on every goddamned corner.
Twelfth and Euclid, his unit under siege,
shots from a second floor apartment. *Gooks
didn't get me; no fuckin' way spooks will.*
Spotted a flare in the window – later
they'd say it was a cigarette – opened
fire. *How could I know about the little
girl, four years, like my own Danielle at home?*

9.

She was thirty-five that birthday, alone
with her almost teenage daughter, while an
army defended the city against
its citizens. Second husband *shacked up
with his girlfriend,* closet missing his clothes.
She'd wept the day she turned thirty, mourning
her vanished girlhood, but no tears today.
Cigarette face looms back from the mirror,
nerve thin; she struck a match, lit another
Marlboro. She could've torched the house; instead,
she ate popcorn I made, studded with pats
of butter, crystals of salt. We took turns
reading to each other, from *Catcher in
the Rye,* feet propped on the coffee table.

Thursday, July 27 and beyond
10.

The fires stop smoldering; troops are withdrawn.
Thousands arrested are booked, charged. Summer
drones on; men in suits hawk their opinions
on TV. "For Sale" signs sprout like a late
crop; the suburbs reap the harvest. I start
junior high, where black kids and white sit
on opposite sides of the lunchroom. Come
winter, my stepfather returns and brings
a gun: *no nigger's gonna bust through my
front door.* In spring, he fires it at my mother,
but misses. When Martin Luther King is
shot, a black girl tells me, *Get away, white
bitch.* I ride the bus downtown to high school,
past torched shells of buildings that stand for years.

1970 ~ Arthur

THE ONE ROSE

Don't leave me alone
for I love only you,
You're the one rose
that's left in my heart.

– "The One Rose,"
by Del Lyon and Lani McIntire

Nights at the piano bar, Chuck's Place for Steak
percussion of ice in glasses, hoarse churn of the blender

"Meet me after work," you'd croon into the receiver
and she always came, sliding onto the stool beside you

Nights blue with neon, gin like thawed diamonds
cigarette embers, smoke rising like regret

You loved the moment when she first walked in, slanting daylight
across dim walls, all eyes on her, best looking woman in the place

Shrimp cocktails and garlic toasts, crocks of spreadable cheese
banter of cops and car dealers, insurance salesmen, jokes and wagers

Your arm around her slim waist, the warm scent of her neck
her dark hair – one lucky sonofabitch

She drank martinis on the rocks with a lemon twist
she'd bite into the peel, savor its bitterness

Later, at home, you would fight, insults hurled
    against much-bruised walls
but in this dark room she was a warm flush on your skin

Requests to Wayne, the pianist, old songs coaxed from fingertips
and you'd raise your voice loudest, eyes full of her

Never again to break
the grip of ice
on a car windshield
in early dark,
nor skid in the direction
of sloping shoulder
on a snow-slicked road,
to leave behind
cold and crime
of Michigan, headlights
aimed toward palm trees,
pull of gulf coast.

She knew I'd dreamt
of it for years: my last
construction job, lock
snapped onto tool box,
heavy, mud-stained boots
kicked off, one final splinter
excised. Trading it all
for days clasped in the sun's
firm handshake, muscles
easing like salt taffy, breeze
giggling like a young girl
in an old man's ear.

I had the car all packed,
her dresses and my shirts
hung like bright flags
on armistice day in the rear
windows. Maps in glove
compartment, a full tank. Frank
would live in our house.
Then she stepped through
the front door, arms crossed,
sudden as a lightning storm:
"I'm not going," all five-
foot-two of her determined.

No "Baby," would persuade
her, no "these old bones
can't take the cold." She grew hard
as the cement beneath her scuffs.
And I could have driven off
and left her, growing smaller
in my rearview mirror until
I disappeared; instead I
unpacked the car, rehung
her dresses into lonely closet.
Then I sat out on the porch step,
watched sun sink into smoke.

CHUCK

They found the parakeet outside
their favorite bar. Escapee
from tidy brick? Sidewalk dweller?
Citron angel? Perhaps wanting
to be found; he was easy to
catch. My stepfather named him Chuck,
not after the lounge, but for his
childhood pet. No doubt about it

Chuck was special. Perched on eyeglass
frames, belly warm against forehead,
he'd peck eyebrows. Or glide to roost
on edge of books held open, or
even newspapers, where he'd
sway perilous as claws gripped thin
sheets of print. Days I was home sick
he'd fly down the long hallway, keep

me company in bed. And he
did not begrudge my stepfather
to scoop him up in giant hands
cover his feathers with kisses.
My stepfather's face would change then,
soften with a tenderness I
did not see otherwise. Perhaps
these bird years were our happiest.

When Chuck got sick, sneezing, huddled
in cage, no vet would see us on
Saturday night; no warming on
the plane of heating pad revived
his musical chirp. By Sunday
morning Chuck was stiff, inert, black
eyes glassy, my stepfather
out back of the garage, weeping.

LIVING ROOM

Most nights you sprawled on the gold
carpet, bare legs sticking out
from your boxers; she, collapsed,
snoring on sofa while cubes
drowned in tall tumblers. Sometimes
I'd drape your naked shoulders
with a rough blanket, turn off
dinner, steak smoking in the
broiler, canned peas blackening
their pot. I'd mix cocoa and
sugar, peanut butter, milk
– grandma's recipe for fudge –
over a low flame, not wait
for it to harden, spoon hot
sludgy sweetness from pan to
mouth till my head spun dizzy
and I could sleep. Beyond my
closed door, the living room still
awake, lamps blazing, TV
burbling a lullaby:
Johnny Carson's signoff bled
into "High Flight,†" a poem
intoned against a backdrop
of silver wings, cloud-filled sky,
close-up on cockpit, broadcast
as if live from your dreams – *And
while with silent lifting mind
I've trod the high untrespassed
sanctity of space, put out
my hand and touched the face of
God* – it blessed your slumbering
form until dissolving to
the National Anthem,
then test patterns until dawn.

---

† A poem by John Gillespie Magee, Jr., a pilot in the Royal Canadian Air Force, who died
in a plane crash in 1941, at the age of nineteen.

GRADUATION

I wasn't there when my grandmother shoved
the guard. I was up onstage in my short
culotte dress I was so proud of, having
lost lots of weight before graduation
suffering over my break-up with Raye.
Even though my gown covered it, even
sweating under black polyester – one
hundred degrees that June, people fanning
their printed programs and rumors a few
fainted – I still felt good in my short dress.
I'd survived high school, and I'd survived love.

None of the thousand graduates in that
class of 'seventy-two was going to stand
for the national anthem. When the band
struck the opening chords, "Oh-oh say can
you see . . ." nobody moved, though our parents
glowered. We deigned rise for "Lift Every
Voice and Sing," compounding our transgression,
and I used the opportunity to
unpeel the sweat-stuck gown from my thighs. Two
white guys passed a joint in our bleachers; just
too damned many of us to monitor.

Which is why we were allowed only
two guests apiece, the auditorium
jammed beyond capacity. Marie was
unmoved by such logistics. I hadn't
seen her in a few years; she rarely left
the house. She was ravaged by that time, gape-
mouthed scowl revealing her remaining yellowed
teeth, brown eyes milky, not quite focusing.
I'd mailed the announcement from some textbook
sense of etiquette, as I'd sent one to
the dad I hadn't seen since I was eight.

Never dreamed she'd appear, clutching the white
card in her stubby fingers, her name scrawled
on the battered envelope. Snarling at
the guard's protests, "I got my invite," built
like a barrel with bandy-legged Adolph
at her side. She must have grown impatient,
feared to miss the moment when I'd rise, cross
stage, only member of her family
to ever do it, so she pushed against
obstruction, years of forcible restraint.
The guard went sprawling. Marie took her seat.

Coming of Age

1. *1972/3* Psych 101

"Now that you're eighteen, you're on your own,"
emancipation sealed with a fifth of Cuervo Gold
presented like keys to the kingdom: your life,
drink it. You rush headlong into

emancipation, succored by a fifth of Cuervo Gold
and a lid of kickass Colombian.
Smoke it, headrush all through class.
Psychology 101. Try to figure out

where to score the next lid of kickass Colombian.
A professor takes you up in his private plane.
Psych 101. He's trying to figure out
how to get you in bed. Nascent feminist,

smoke dope in the professor's private plane,
watch the city plummet far beneath you.
Amusing, how he wants to bed this nascent feminist,
plunge his twin-engine into your milky skies.

Watch the world spin further and further from you.
The textbook is full of lies. It tries to
plunge its binary opposites into your milky ego;
more than once you slam out of class in protest.

Textbook lies about how women try to
construct themselves out of scraps of culture.
You slam out of class to protest spare ribs,
hand-me-down identities, projected pathologies of men.

Construct yourself from scraps of culture:
Stoned Soul Picnic, Cries and Whispers, Atlas Shrugged.
Shrug off passivity, projected pathologies of men.
No one imagines your authenticity.

Boogie On Reggae Woman, Carnal Knowledge, Rubyfruit Jungle
You scavenge for keys to a new kingdom, your life.
Who will imagine your authenticity?
Now that you're eighteen, you're on your own.

2. *1974* Lunch Truck

At four a.m., wakefulness
has barely begun to be
disentangled from dreaming
blankets. You rise in darkness,
sleep follows all day, faithful
as shadow. Breath fogs, silvers
in black air, rime crystals hatch
windshield; steel patches of ice
on which truck wheels spin, as in
dreams where you run,
                              go nowhere.
Even the sugar scent of
crullers seems narcotic, and
the slosh of pale coffee in
giant urns. Spigots gush for
men nursing hangovers, lined
faces red veined, wind chapped.
You never master the jest
and banter, sports scores, dirty
jokes. Your smile for them vacant
as a sleepwalker, eyes on
flat moonscape of construction
sites, snow on stacked lumber,
concrete tracts of car dealerships,
auto parts stores.
                        Cellophane
crackles around egg salad,
tuna fish, ham – triangles
stacked in refrigerated
display, white bread or brown. Bags
of potato chips, chilled cans
of pop. Breakfast bleeds into
lunch, candy bars at half past
nine, Danish well past noon; these
men eat whenever you toot

your horn. Motown on scratchy
radio, you steer pot-holed
highways, gray slush at the shoulders,
sneaking a joint between
industrial park and Ray's
Body Shop.
              You drift through days,
refuse to think of green lawns,
maple-lined walkways, ivied
brick of campus walls, that hushed
artificial world
your mother coveted. A world
you fled, day of first snow,
eyes on window, not test
sheets where alphabets drifted,
flurried, melted before they touched
earth. Lies melted from memory,
you stood, slammed door of
examination hall. That
world traded for "freedom;" too
late you learned that freedom smells
of bland mustard,
                   doughnut grease.
At shift's end, scrub rock salt from
fenders, drain urns into gutter,
count worn, grimy bills from
apron pocket. Four p.m.,
pale sun already surrendered.
Tell yourself there is still
day left, still time to shop for
lipstick, catch a movie, hell,
read a book, but before you
can unlace your muddy boots,
shed thermal underwear, sleep
finally wins the day-long
argument, flattens you with
a sucker punch, lays its claim.

INHERITED TRAIT

The art of stealing sleeping pills
from my lover's medicine chest
is like a spell, the flintstruck will
to transmute seeping, needy flesh
into desireless bone, to pass
invisible through walls and be gone.

Summer. Threat of rain is always
in the air. My apartment stinks
of mice; I hear them scuttle
behind baseboards while I don't
sleep. Red wine mingles with the taste
of blood against my tongue. Fingers

trace the hollows of my hips. I
stare through attic windows at a
merciless sky. Slipping down, those
pills smack of graying blackboards. Want
my lover to find me when she
gets back from Pennsylvania,

find me and be sorry. I am
too bulky to pass through walls, swelled
and sodden with grief. My waitress
uniform hangs in the tiny
bathroom, rinsed out after the last
shift – puffed sleeve blouse, apron, drooping

L'Eggs. It's because I waitress that
I want to die. "Miss, this coffee
tastes bitter . . ." It's not just the bombed
out gene of terminal despair;
it's destiny I can't fulfill,
mission thwarted, dream deferred. Fire

starved for fuel, smothered by snow, ash,
muted expectation. Marie
chose to combust rather than snuff
herself out; did she too gasp for
oxygen in airless rooms? Some
one does perish in that Sunday

attic; still, an ember stirs, glows.
Someone is reborn; folks call her
"Phoenix," leave her tips under
yolk-coated plates. These pity coins
will multiply in a glass jar;
to let go is the only way

to keep faith. Jet plane propels her
to city of red-hot angels;
"Buenvenidos, señorita."
Untempered sun extends its tongues,
licks 'til she ignites, home at last
in her incendiary light.

EXILE

1.

I couldn't survive the Midwest – meatloaf
and Miracle Whip, weak coffee, Jello
salads. Softball and gray skies, Friday night
bars. Flag on the Fourth of July. The dearth
of art films. Forests cleared for farmland, green
fields plowed under for industrial parks.
Jobs in diners, data processing, used
car lots. All that white skin. Mute acceptance
of weather. My despair stuck out like a
tight red dress in church. I craved spice and strong
rhythms, my snake tongue poised to strike. I longed
for sun to burn through skin, eyes that would meet
mine. I needed an edge to teeter on,
a cracking ledge above a vast unknown.

2.

When the ground shakes in California,
birds fall silent, know the territory
over which they swoop is rearranged, land
scrambled, and trees pluck up their roots. Fissures
spit up thousand-year-old dust – Indian
bones – devour our puny notions of
stability. What's buried is released,
blown hot by Santa Ana winds against
our eyes. Heart's hammer eases, we who came
here for the jolt, for earth's shock therapy.
I imagine walking with Marie, sun
freckling our shoulders, along the curled
hem of the Pacific. Her gazed has cleared,
her grimace soothed. She seldom trembles now.

—៷៷—

Diaspora

It wasn't like war –
the enemy come
up quick and slit your
throat with his knife, sky
spins black till you
travel the road of bones.

Great-grandmother told
how spring currents brought
pale men with cook pots,
arrow tips sharper
than stone. We called them
agnonha, "iron

people"; we traded
soft pelts for their hard
metal till beaver
disappeared from our
forest. From then on
we had no home; so

many walked the road
of bones, our numbers
halved by spotted fever,
guns exploding from
the boats of pale men,
then our fingers learned

to grasp the trigger.
Like fingers splayed, our
clans dispersed to lands
beyond our language –
children scattered to
Gahoendoe isle,

Michilimackinac;
their spawn exiled to
Jeune Lorette, Detroit –
rough syllables like
stones to scrape away
memory. Somewhere

my blood ticks inside
the veins of one who
has never heard my
name. Tell me, Spirit,
in what lost tongue do
my descendants dream?

LETTER TO MARIE

Nobody told me you were dead
until the red-eye from Los Angeles
touched down onto gray
frozen runway. Christmas in Detroit.

I stumbled sleepless from cabin
dazed but tense, anticipating
how my mother's hungry
eyes would stalk the deplaned

passengers, anxious to recognize
me, alert for changes in hair
color, length; my stepfather
beside her, mouth aching,

dental plates ground against
raw gums. Swallowed by her
hug, familiar rush of Charlie
cologne surrounding me; his

awkward off-hand greeting; her
brave broken smile. She waited
till he'd gone to fetch my luggage,
battered blue suitcase that had once

been hers. Then: *Grandma
Young died. Three days ago.
Funeral yesterday. Your dad's
upset.* I stood blinking

in fluorescent air; a night spent
sitting up, downing scotch, dozing
to engines' drone had dulled
me: *who were these people*

*who would keep your death
from me?* I counted telephone
poles, imagined them stretched
from Great Lakes to Pacific, electric

impulse leaping across wire
like flame. Snuffed out. No sputtered
protest would unpeel those days, settle
me beside your coffin, let me stroke

your fallen jowl. *I kept
some of her jewelry,* my mother
offered, *thought you might want
it.* When we reached Baggage

Claim, I hugged my stepfather,
first time in years. His red face
reddened deeper still; we followed
his sagging shoulders to the car.

The freeway journey silent, pale sun
glinting off iced branches. My tongue
untrained to twist around the rosary you would
have wanted; this poem my only prayer.

BEQUEST

It was her jewelry they brought for me
after her heart, like an exhausted match,
sputtered and flared out, a cigar box stuffed
with smaller boxes, gilt lids chipped with age.

Nests of white tissue housed her finery,
dimestore treasures, never worn, a child's cache
cheap metals gleaming innocent, enough
rhinestones to satisfy a poor girl's urge

for movie magic, star-struck fantasy.
A necklace of blue stones, blank eyes that catch
and hold the light; its brassy setting left
a bruise of green against my throat, the smudge

betraying it as make-believe, a flimsy
fetish. The prism pendants she would filch
from Woolworth's cast their rainbow glints to drift
across scarred walls in my room at the edge

of this continent, far from the city
where they'd first tempted her. And I still flinch
at losing her twin snake bracelets, the cuffed
spiral on each wrist a tensile bondage,

their gold too bright; each pair of verdigris
stones set in hollow eye sockets kept watch.
I felt dangerous as Eve when she scoffed
at God's demands, bared herself to knowledge

in the serpent's grasp, tasted of the tree,
succumbed to lust. And doesn't God punish
all who follow in her steps? No shrift
absolved my grandmother's sin, left to scavenge

rough salvation in psychiatry,
her every strangled prayer met with reproach.
My own penance with this: a petty theft
deprived me of those bracelets; some teenage

vandal pocketed her legacy –
the coiled power, all that she could snatch.
Still I've kept their wisdom; she would have laughed
to know, these long years after, how their strange

tacky allure shines yet in memory,
their hissing haunts my breath, green eyes bewitch,
my wrist bones naked, sheer skin gone soft,
blue veins seethe venom under cartilage.

CIRCLES

Women in circles sometimes we bleed together turn our hair the color of flame Marie underground with worms still burning we sit in circles stories bleed from bottomless mouths we are journeyers exiles motherless daughters turning our worlds upside down we ravage boundaries resist confinement turn our lives into art into myth dream Elsba dreaming in her cancer bed in circles our revolutions shake the ground inside us confess transform we shed skin claim this serpent power for our own seize reviled names of women castoff body parts Ruth teeters on the precipice of loneliness we cradle our vulvas bare breasts encircle madness burn inside it flame hisses confesses flame anneals myth of dreaming earth bleeding breasts of motherless daughters bleed across thresholds of freedom dream a revolution of snake mothers claim a castoff lineage cradle Marie Elsba Ruth in circles of lonely cancer madness bottomless beds of flame and light we sit in circles and we listen

In State

It has snowed all day,
tires skidding on asphalt
the whole way from Detroit
to North Baltimore, Ohio,
Christmas day, my mother weeping,
grandpa in the back seat
next to me, his mute grief
crowding the car, my ribs
pressed to the arm rest,
even you, at the wheel, silent.

The tiny town is holiday
hushed, streets unplowed, everyone
tucked in their tidy homes,
sealed under accumulating
blankets, shops closed
except the funeral parlor,
bland beige rooms
and polished wood,
the scent of pine,
lowered voices and waiting.

Three days ago I awoke
past noon in my lover's bed
in California, my cells aching
with a malady I could not
pinpoint, head cottony, bones
heavy as if yoked to an unseen
weight. In a dream I said,
"It's not something entering,
it's something leaving."
Next morning, Elsba was dead.

The viewing begins at dusk;
unremembered relatives
arrive in pressed suits, country
haircuts; galoshes tramp
slush on the welcome mat.
My sleepless flight from L.A.,

the tense car trip in a Christmas
blizzard, an endless afternoon
confined in mortuary chairs fray
the edges of my faked smile.

I have to get out, I know
suddenly, wrap myself in grandma's
mouton coat, the air
bites my cheeks, the raw
tip of my nose, flakes
land on my collar
to die. I light a joint,
lungs fill with smoke
and frost, tears ice
in the corner of my eyes.

Strings of lights burn
their colors into pillowed
drifts; farther down Main Street
one door glows golden.
A bar, and I enter
gratefully, the only patron
at dinner hour on Christmas
night. I slide onto
a stool; scotch shivers
through my esophagus.

The bartender asks no
questions, leaves me alone
to muse on Christmas
in Los Angeles, palm trees
bending in the wind, red strands
of tail lights on rain-slick
freeways. I think of my lover,
of the jade plant that blooms
beyond her bedroom window.
I spot a phone booth

in the corner, take comfort
in a plan to call her,
but before I can dig for change,
the door bangs open and you
bluster in, snow in your hair,
collar hiked around your ears.
You claim the seat beside
me, "Martini with a twist."
"I had to get out of there,"
I tell you, and you nod.

We drink in a companionable
silence. The amber light
of the barroom seems to cradle
us. Tiny bulbs blink amongst
the line of bottles; juke box
brings us Nat King Cole.
You adored my grandma,
mistook the gentleness
with which she disapproved
of you for love. "A saint,"

you call her now, and raise
your glass. I wonder if you think
about Marie, dead one year,
but you don't say. The funeral
home is crowded with good people
gathered to pay last respects –
farmers who live by weather
and by prayer, who love
the flag and a big meal after
church on Sundays.

They've never gambled away
the mortgage payment, dropped
LSD on a freeway overpass,
shoplifted, cheated on
their mates, sliced their wrists.
They've never set their house

on fire, or danced with snakes.
That's why we're here, ordering
another round, while my mother,
gracious in her grief, shakes every hand.

ARTISTRY

1978 ~ Ruth

Color bleeds from her dissolving house – pink
kitchen molten, green living room fluxed; gold
ring joins the first one, discarded in dark
drawer. Bed shorn of comfort leeches white.

New apartment drab, suburban. Eggshell
walls, gray spectrum of TV. Carport. Trash
compactor. Black telephone. Forty-six,
the first time in her life she's lived alone.

Her only daughter – hair glows henna
under California sun – exhorts
her to take up the palette, paint fissured
walls of her life in brilliant chroma.

But after work, silent rooms drain pigment,
render nights long, bleached bone, ashen as ghosts.

2000 ~ Terry

One morning the old cat leaves, hobbles on
spindled legs into eternity. Takes
with her the puling cries for tuna, hairs
that carpeted my black sweaters, steady
gaze of her topaz eyes. I'm forty-five;
two rings abandoned in a velvet box.
When the key turns and my door swings open,
dark silence greets me like the breath of god.

When my mother married for the third time,
I sneered and sent no presents, sure she'd failed
to grasp the art of solitude. Now TV
flickers blue against my sinking face;
as inspiration falters, pigments reek,
the palette grown so dreary to my eyes.

FRANK

My stepfather never
spoke his brother's name
without a sneer,
without accompanying
epithets:
faggot, fairy, fruit
or *fucking queer.*
Adolph had done them
both as kids
but Frank had *liked* it.

He never sat at our table,
no call on holidays;
Frank hovered beyond
our shuttered windows,
a forgotten ghost,
his despised life
lived offstage, vagabond
of seedy bars,
furtive gropings
in unlit corners.

Years fell like ashes
from a cigarette.
My stepfather haunted
other women's beds
until he gained
his fourth divorce,
claimed that's what he'd wanted,
never to rewed.
He lived alone in rented rooms
that stunk of strangers.

When Adolph died
my stepfather reclaimed
his youngest brother.
I'm told Frank had become
like Howard Hughes:
wore only pajamas,
refused to leave the house.
Still, they'd come from the same mother.
Frank was: *someone to watch TV*
with, someone to cook for.

ELOISE

In 1894, the Wayne County Poorhouse got a new name.
Freeman B. Dickerson, president of the County board
overseeing the poor, renamed the facility Eloise,
after his five-year-old daughter. . . . Eloise Hospital
for the Insane.

> — "Eloise: the poorhouse that became an asylum"
> by Mary Bailey, *The Detroit News*

1800

Once, mules pulled furrows into the skin
of this ground each springtime. Dirt swollen
with rain opened to the scattering
of seed; corn, beans, sugar beets pressed up
against the weight of overcast sky.

1825

Cabin built from split trunks of felled trees
squats in the field; carved sign above door
reads Black Horse Tavern. Wagons trundle
the rough road; heavy boots tromp earth's worn
face, her parched mouth gagging on spilt malt.

1839

Wayne County buys the land; Black Horse turns
to Poorhouse. Two days by stagecoach from
Detroit; the ragged, dirty, drunk and
penniless are scuttled out of sight,
forced to plant themselves in this hard soil.

1841

Black horse stampedes the dreams of Biddy
Hughes, the first mental patient. Kept chained
above the pigsty, she shrieks, stamps the
dust. Committed by family, she
stays fifty-eight years until she dies.

1869

New roofs are needed to shelter the
proliferating poor, the mad; more
land choked with houses of misery.
Beneath the earth stir pale, restless bones;
all night they howl at the trembling moon.

1894

Just five, Blonde Eloise has never
played in the clay dirt of grounds that bear
her name. White dress unsmirched by grass stain,
plump knees unskinned. Dreams undisturbed by
round vowels – *El-ohh-eese* – puled in dread.

1910

Tuberculars are housed in open
air, under the stretch of canvas tents;
feet shuffle over stubbled grass that
browns and dies. Percussive hacking joins
the squalled chorus from the mental wards.

1939

Eight thousand now call this plot home. *The*
residents rise at seven a.m.
and go to bed at seven-thirty
p.m. Between times they sit and stare
at the wall, at their feet, at . . . windows.

1945

Harsh soil can yield a bountiful crop;
seventy-five buildings sprout across
the land: Fire department. Police force.
Bakery. Laundry. Morgue – everything
planted must be someday harvested.

1962

After a jolt of voltage charges
through her nerve endings, Marie drifts through
the corridors; for days her feet don't
touch ground. The whispering voices go
silent; now she's ready to go home.

1981

The earth goes fallow; buildings fall. Gates
are chained; concrete foundations ruptured
by persistent weeds. Thin sunlight spills
onto cracked, bare walls. The bones rattle
and turn. Wasps circle in empty rooms.

1983 ~ Terry

LETTER TO ARTHUR

I've been living in California
almost seven years, yet
I'm still afraid to let
you have my address.
It's not just paranoia:

ever since the divorce
I've been hearing stories
like the one in which you shot
a Puerto Rican man
who tried to steal your TV

or the time you smashed
the window with a rifle butt,
shoved my mother down
the basement stairs
when she refused to take you back.

I begged her to move,
shield herself from threatening
phone calls, late night break-ins;
I begged her not to tell
you I was coming to visit

but she never listened.
When a friend drove me
in from the airport, I spotted
your car in my mother's driveway;
we circled and circled the block.

I made my friend drop me
at The Waffle House, air sweet
with maple syrup, then called
my mother, swore, "I'm not coming
there until he's gone."

Hours later, she retrieved me
from a corner booth, my belly
sour with cold coffee.
When I was finally curled
on the sofa in her living room, smelling

her familiar perfume, the phone
shattered the evening:
you were coming back, you vowed
to hurt me if she still rebuffed you.
I knew you'd do it

so I bullied her, "Either we check
into a motel tonight, or you can drive
me right back to the airport."
We spent three days on lounge
chairs by the pool at Holiday Inn.

Back in California, I moved, made sure
you never had my address. I live now
with my lover, our two cats, and ghosts
that snake dance through dreams
of blasted childhood – a crowded house.

Of you, I tell myself, "You're lucky
not to hear from him." Still I can't
forget those early Saturday mornings
at Eastern Market, how you'd shake
me from my teenage stupor

drive through dawn to roam
the farmer's stalls, your delight in fresh
ears of corn, ripe tomatoes. Or how
you bailed me out when I was busted
at thirteen for shoplifting; leaving

the police station you said, "Let's
not tell your mother." Or that quiet
drink we shared in an empty bar
in the middle of a Christmas blizzard
the day they buried grandma.

It's that lingering taste of scotch
that lures me to my typewriter,
the blue portable my lover gave
me, the one I'd named Victory,
and my fingers tap the words

"**Dear Dad**" though I never
think of you that way, always
"Mac" or "my stepfather."
I know you prefer "Dad," recall
that time in high school

when I introduced you to my date,
"This is my stepfather,"
and your forehead reddened
and my mother told me later
how you punched the wall.

Such a careful bridge of words
I'm trying to build over murky
waters, a twisted span
from my humanity to yours.
Perilous crossing, much left

unsaid. "**Haven't seen you
in a long time** . . ." but no mention
of why. "**I'm doing well, quit drinking**,"
I confide, but dare not invoke
your daily fifths of gin.

"I'm a lesbian," I find the courage
to peck, but my nerve fails
when it comes to recounting
those afternoons in steamy bathrooms,
a little girl, her naked stepfather.

**"Things happened that hurt me,
and hurt me still . . ."** is the best
I can manage. Keys hammer
their tiny fists into the page. Then:
"I remember the good times too," and thank

you for those market trips, the way
you'd bring me hot fudge sundaes
when I was sick in bed, how
you cried when Chuck, our parakeet,
died, buried him in back of the garage.

Three times I type it up, each
word scrutinized. The earlier
drafts become wadded balls
ricocheted off the lip of the waste
basket. I consult my lover,

"Are you sure that doesn't sound
too mean? Well, is it too wimpy?"
until, spent, I slip the pages
in an envelope, scrawl my work
address in the upper left.

What I want, of course,
is for you to meet me in the middle
of this rickety bridge, stretched
between betrayal and forgiveness,
to feel its sway beneath our feet,

gaze into thick green water,
risk the plunge. I want a correction
key for the past, want memory
to flow clear, unsludged, below.
Goddamn it, I want a father.

"**Hope you'll write back,**" my closing line,
"**I love you.**" Some weeks later
an envelope arrives at my office,
six sheets dashed in your impatient
hand. You do not come to stand

beside me, suspended above
the depths; instead, you menace
the silty bank, cast sharp stones
at shadows underneath
the surface of the water:

Your mother took everything I had,
she locked me out, stole the house,
the furniture; I ended up with my clothes
and your 12" TV. And I never had
to drink, just liked to, and I guess

there is a difference. And how *we have*
to take the bitter with the sweet.
You barely glance in my direction,
and the railing comes loose
in my clenched hands. Above me, lightning

cracks, leaves the air singed.
In this way I learn the limits
of forgiveness, and though this bridge
I've built might lead me to the other side,
you won't follow.

I will write you again, because
I cannot turn away completely
from this river. That letter will return,
unopened, "Cannot Deliver. Addressee
unknown. No forwarding address."

GIN

Cards slap table, ice clicks
against sweating glass. A
room away, TV drones,
joins with fan's insect hum,
clock tick, eats at silence.

In kitchen, my mother
keeps score on envelopes,
my hand full of aloof
Queens; their blank eyes meet mine.
Soupy dark crowds windows.

She drops the King on Hearts
on wood-grain Formica:
my draw. Sips her drink. My
hand resists pairing. She
taught me this game, tactics:

how to build runs – King, Queen,
Jack – to knock early, to
remember, withhold what
my opponent craves. When
I visit, every few

years, we pull out the worn
deck, hunker behind fanned
cards – those faded hunting
dogs still chasing through woods –
elude each other's eyes.

DEVIL'S NIGHT

At each fire there were crowds of onlookers . . . civilian
thrill seekers from the suburbs, many of them on their
one annual trip to the city . . . augmented by people
who had come from all over the United States, Europe,
and the Far East to participate in Devil's Night,
the fire buff's Superbowl.

— Ze'ev Chafets, *Devil's Night and Other True Tales of Detroit*

Late October. Red leaves drift, crackle
and blacken, consumed in bonfires. Smoke
clings to the ribbed hems of sweaters, sleeves
of flannel shirts. We carry its scent
into the house, odor of cooling
afternoons, cider and caramel
apples, the peppery smell of ash.

At thirteen, the eve of Halloween
was time for devilment: eggs hurled at
screen doors, yolk welding to mesh; ribbons
of toilet paper strewn across hedge
and tree; "FUCK," "SHIT" scrawled on windows in
Dial soap. Fevered running on night
pavement, dodging street lamps, delinquent.

Bad boys bragged of lunch bags set afire,
left on step, doorbell rung. Homeowners –
racing onto porch to stamp out flames,
the bag full of dog shit, stench released
by urgent feet – would stare into blank
street alive with laughing shadows. Then,
it seemed the worst prank one could play.

That was before Detroit was christened
Murder City. Before white suburbs
fortressed against black metropolis.
Before the Arab oil embargo
siphoned the tank of car culture. And

the Lions moved to Pontiac. Before
Renaissance Towers loomed empty.

Who knows who dropped the first match, soaked
rags in gasoline? It might have been
spontaneous combustion: three days
in nineteen-eighty-three, over eight
hundred fires bloom. Abandoned houses
blister, succumb; flames enfold the husks
of idle factories. Black sky glows.

Now, an annual event. News crews
jostle with fire fighters, sightseers,
cops, and worried neighbors, hosing their
roofs while the world gawks. Two thousand miles
away, my skin is singed, hair catches,
ignites. Detroit burns inside me; some
pain can only be relieved by blaze.

Fire kindles the imagination;
drab streets of boarded windows, weedy
lots, transformed into scintilla
of sparks, turning to gold the cold blue
air. Abandoned rooms ignite, crack vials
melt. Ghetto almost holy in flame
light; the pyros priests who purify.

THE DEAD STEPFATHER

1.

You are already dead when I am told
about your fall on New Year's eve, skull cracked
like an egg against Detroit pavement, yolk
seeping into gray matter. How it took
six days to find your next-of-kin, daughter
who said, "Pull the plug."
                              I was your daughter
once; I'm no one now. Thirty-five years since
you brought me red balloons the night you came
to woo my mother, seventeen since we
last spoke. Those years between, a history
of breakage – bones and glass and brittle vows –
the fragile membrane torn, pieces scattered.
No way for me to claim your death; I'm just
the divorced step-daughter, irrelative.

2.

If there had been a funeral, incense
would have smelled like gunpowder, gasoline,
and gin, pews crowded with barflies, aging
soldiers, used car salesmen, ghosts of children
clutching red balloons. We would have sung "The
One Rose," in lugubrious chorus, then
shared a stiff drink all around.
                                  There was no
service. Three weeks your body stiffened at
the morgue till your daughter found the cheapest
way to burn you, then dispatch your ashes
to a remote grave. Fuck good-byes. In dreams,
I swim with you across a frozen sea,
fathomless blue; we fight the tide, dodge ice
floes white as shells, until you reach the shore.

CHILDLESS

The future soaked each month into white fiber
my shed potential leaves a rust-red stain

this womb as useless as an empty basket
unfilled by stars or moonlight, unbitten fruit

I didn't come here to be a vessel, nor
forge the next sad link in a chain of gin fumes

and broken furniture. No one will preserve
my photographs, collect my garnet ring, my

necklace of bottle caps. But neither will
I trample the soft petals of children, bruise

their unformed bodies with my fingerprints. Let
red eggs swirl in a porcelain bowl, wash out

to sea. Let that future burn, let white ash fly
into white sky. Let new myth begin with me.

Two Roses

Arm in arm, they amble down the street,
mother and daughter, in ancient housedresses.

The daughter, probably sixty, hair dyed a brassy orange,
calls out her admiration for the roses I stand clipping;

her voice, glazed with cigarettes, brash, unsentimental
as an aging hooker, reminds me of my grandmother,

the one who played bingo, the one with jack-o-lantern teeth,
whose brown eyes deadened into gray from shock treatment.

It is late afternoon, and the roses spread and stretch their petals
to the waning light, scarlet and coral, mauve and blush.

"Do you want one?" I ask, as they start to pass.
"Would you like a rose?" I wave my scissors

as they nod, surprised. I choose one, poised to cut,
but the flame-haired daughter knows just what she wants,

the darkest crimson, the one whose petals dry to black.
"Be careful of the thorns," I tell her. Without my invitation

she consults the white-haired crone, "¿Tu quieres? ¿Cual color?"
One nut-brown finger points in the direction of

a grandiflora, striated gold and red as a tequila sunrise.
One slice, and it is hers.

Breath of Fire

Room dim but for a candled glow,
we sit on mats upon the floor.
Floor is ocean, mats are rafts
on which we travel time, then drift.

We know the body is the house
of consciousness; we know our cells
are portals for transmutation:
matter to energy to light.

Practice unfurls us, unwinds coiled
strands: lineage, identity,
tight constrictions that separate
one from another, bone from soul.

My grandmother struck matches to
expose the immolating flare
that burned within, and to see who
might spark back, who might light her way.

Now I close my eyes and pant, breathe
fire. Kundalini snake ascends
laddered spine, ignites the crown. This
is how I burn my way to god.

POEM TO THE DETROIT RIVER

Detroit – where the weak are killed and eaten.

    – T-shirt slogan, circa 1990

. . . the 33 year old woman . . . leapt to her death . . .
from a crowded bridge that . . . connects Detroit . . . with its
famous island park, Belle Isle. She was trying to escape the
300-pound man whose car she had accidentally bumped into.
According to police, the man had smashes her car windows
with a tire iron, dragged her from the vehicle – stripping off
most of her clothes in the process – slammed her against the
hood of her car and pounded her with his fists. Deletha Word
. . . could not swim . . . She jumped into the water 40 feet below.

    – James Ricci, *Los Angeles Times* [August 31, 1995]

The road to the afterlife – There was . . . a river that had only
one bridge across it . . . This bridge was guarded by a dog that
jumped at souls and made many of them fall into the river and drown.

    – Bruce G. Trigger, *The Huron: Farmers of the North*

          Not really a river at all,
          but a handshake between two Great
          Lakes, Huron stretching to embrace
          Erie in its green-gray grasp. You
          stitch the liquid boundary of
          a city dismantling itself,
          bricks unmortared, spires sagging, burnt
          out structures razed to open field.
          Prairies returning here, foxtails
          and chicory, Queen Anne's lace sways;
          tumbleweeds amble down Woodward
          Avenue, blow past fire hydrants,
          storefronts and rusted Cadillacs.

          You are the mirror into which
          we plunge. Towers of a stillborn
          renaissance bend to admire their

vacant beauty; automobiles
built in Mexico catch the chrome
reflection of your waves. They speed
across the bridge to the island
whose willows spill their tears against
your breast. Darkness closes our eyes;
the park empties, bridge bears a chain
of headlights. Perfume of exhaust
drifts over your blackened currents;
cars jostle for their place in line.

Not the fist of one man but
the sucker punch of a city
taking scrappy pride in its bruised
countenance. One bumper kisses
another like gunshot; the town
explodes. You swallow the blood of
a woman's shattered cheekbone, pressed
to metal hood, scorched by engine's
heat. *Who wanna buy some of dis
bitch – she got to pay fo' my car.*
So naked in our headlights. Her
manicure rakes bridge's edge – some
bystanders yell, *Jump!* – she lets go.

You catch the women who plummet
from the sky, seeking safety in
your watery clutches. They root
inside your skin; lungs swell with your
essence. Arms wrestle the eddies
but finally surrender, give
themselves fully. Guardian dog
of the bridge leans muzzle over
the rail, slavering. The whole pack
looks down, red eyes gleaming. She's lost
to us, but we hear her singing
forever in our dreams, gurgled
lullaby for this drowned city.

1999 ~ Terry

MATCH GIRL

She rubbed another match against the wall; . . . in the brightness
[her] old grandmother stood clear and shining . . . "Grandmother!"
cried the child. "Oh, take me with you!" . . . And she hastily rubbed
the whole bundle of matches, for she wished to hold her
grandmother fast.
   . . . in the corner . . . sat the poor girl with red cheeks and smiling
mouth, frozen to death on the last evening of the Old Year . . .
stiff and cold, with the matches of which one bundle was burned.
   "She wanted to warm herself," the people said.

      —"The Little Match Girl" by Hans Christian Anderson

My grandmother huddles between worlds,
in Purgatory's endless waiting
room; all the magazines are old, most
of the pages torn out. Lysol scrapes
the nostrils with a sharp fingernail,
barely masks the stench of sweat. Clock hands
stretch forward like wings, as in escape.
Ashtrays overflow, but the matches
never spark. On a busted TV
filled with snow, a tired announcer drones
the details of Marie's crimes, always
gets them wrong. Her head droops heavy as
oratorio; full notes hammer
her temples. She's chosen me to tell
her story, spar with god for her soul.
I dwell in the City of Angels
and am not afraid of god. The match
ends of my fingertips ignite.

At the hem of the Pacific, I
try to warm myself on the flame of
a woman's smile. "You've got soul," her dark
eyes approve. "Detroit burns in my veins,"
I promise her, "freeway with no speed
limit." My heart a junkyard of wrecked
Chevy's. Rhythm and blues steams up from

the pavement of my skin, a summer
day, the city blazing. Assembly
line of my hips, honky-tonk of my
lips. This lover calls me "Cherry Pie"
but turns her light away. Grandmother's
madness snakes through my brain; too many
times I've scorched my eyelids in my urge
to burn. "Hasta la vista, baby,"
I whisper, while god dons his boxing
gloves. Matches sputter, flare like dying
stars. Marie reaches for my scarred hand.

ACKNOWLEDGMENTS

I wish to thank my mother, Ruth Tackabery, and my stepsister, Judy Collon-Emmons, for sharing with me their memories. I am especially grateful to Sally Charette, whose research assistance proved so fruitful throughout the writing of this book, and to Erin Shannon and Renee Simms for additional research assistance.

I wish to thank editor Elaine Katzenberger and poet Michelle T. Clinton for their thoughtful consideration and discussion of this work. I am especially appreciative of Kate Gale and Mark Cull for their continued commitment to my work, and Kim Dower (Kim-from-L.A.) for her energy and enthusiasm. I am deeply grateful to the current and past members of the Women's Poetry Project, including especially Megan Black, Ana Castañon, Sheryl Cobb, Cheryl Dullabaun, Yvonne Estrada, Mary Cecille Gee, Robin Podolsky, Kathryn Robyn, Sue Scheibler, Pat Viera, and Alicia Vogl Saenz, and the members of my Monday Night Writers Group – Jacqueline de Angelis, Julia Gibson, Lynette Prucha-Chavez, and Noelle Sickels – for their encouragement and their insightful and generous feedback on the work. Thank you to Gwin Wheatley for her unflagging belief in and efforts on behalf of my work, and to Carole Carp for additional support.

I also want to thank Sasha Marcus, in whose living room so many of these poems were generated.

This work is indebted to the scholarship of Nancy Bonvillain and Bruce G. Trigger, whose published works about the Wendat were important resources.

This publication could not have come to pass without the generous support of Pat Alderete and Mary-Linn Hughes, Amgen, Anonymous, Nancy Conn, Susan Crespi, Julia Gibson, Sondra Hale, Matt Knight, Ellen Lazares, Linda Preuss, Leslie Stone, M. Gwin Wheatley, and Maggie Wilkinson. Your willingness to support alternative publishing helps to insure that literature remains vibrant, diverse, and experimental.

"City of Salt" was previously published in *Crab Orchard Review,* Vol. 6, No. 2, Spring-Summer 2001; "Drive-In" was previously published in *The Lesbian Review of Books,* Vol. V, No. 4, Summer 1999; "Gin" was previously published in a slightly different form in *Black Slip,* Clothespin Fever Press, 1992; "The Dead Stepfather" was previously published in *The Jacaranda Review,* 1996. All are reprinted with the permission of the author.

Terry Wolverton is the author of *Insurgent Muse,* a memoir; *Bailey's Beads,* a novel; and two collections of poetry, *Black Slip* and *Mystery Bruise.* Her fiction, poetry, essays, and drama have been published in periodicals internationally, including *Glimmer Train Stories, Zyzzyva, Many Mountains Moving,* and *The Jacaranda Review,* and widely anthologized.

She has also edited several successful compilations, including *His: brilliant new fiction by gay men* and *Hers: brilliant new fiction by lesbians,* volumes 1, 2, and 3; and *Lesbian Fiction At the Millennium* and *Gay Fiction At the Millennium.*

In 1997, she founded Writers at Work, a center for creative writing in Los Angeles, where she teaches several weekly workshops in fiction and poetry. She is the recipient of numerous awards for her artistic and community contributions, and is a certified instructor of Kundalini Yoga.